I'm Glad I Was Adopted

A JOURNEY TO WHOLENESS AND FAITH

ROXANNE TAYLOR

ISBN (eBook): 978-1-967120-42-0

ISBN (Paperback): 978-1-967120-43-7

Library of Congress Control Number: 2026904567

Cover art by Tia Rigsby.

Author headshot courtesy of Finkbeiner Photography.

Published by Indie Christian Book in Bloomington, Illinois, U.S.A.

www.indiechristianbook.com

A mother's love is like no other, and Rosemary loved me unconditionally until the day she died. For a good portion of my childhood, she was a single mom who sacrificed, making sure that I would have a childhood filled with dance lessons, concerts, even a summer drama program. She did everything she could to be sure I understood that I was always wanted and loved. Her special nickname for me was P.T., which stood for Precious Treasure. Growing up, I didn't always agree with her decisions and advice, but eventually I came to realize she only wanted what was best for me.

With tremendous love and gratitude, I dedicate my first book to my mother, who invested her life to raise me. Her prayers protected and carried me through many tough times, and I am forever indebted to her for giving me a home full of her love and dedication.

Contents

Prologue

PUZZLE PIECES: WHY
YOUR STORY MATTERS

SOME TIME HAD PASSED after locating my birth family when I began to realize that pieces of my story were beginning to fit together like a puzzle.

All of us have spent hours attempting to assemble jigsaw puzzles. The pieces have irregular shapes. But when they all fit together, they reveal the big picture. It is usually a strikingly beautiful landscape or cute puppies or kittens.

Perhaps our lives are like puzzles.

Of course there are parts of our lives that are not always beautiful or cute. I promise mine wasn't always a wonderful life. Often the puzzles of our lives are littered with difficult and painful experiences. I have found these experiences shape us into the strong people we eventually become.

I would like to invite you to join me as I share my adoption story, one that has unfolded over the last seventy-one years. I have come to understand some valuable lessons, ones that may help you in your own life as an adoptee.

It was before the internet was even invented that I decided to search for my birth family. That made locating information extremely difficult. I used mail or phone calls to do research and to ask for advice. Shockingly, in 1991, my written request to a judge here in Florida to unseal my adoption records was approved. That approval made it possible to find details about my birth family. Some years later, in May of 2004, I met with a private investigator to see if he could assist me in my search. Within just fifteen hours of our meeting, he located my birth family.

Slowly I started to learn the details of my adoption, and the big picture began to appear. My newfound aunt bluntly told me how lucky I was to have been adopted! It didn't take me long to realize that she was right. From the moment of conception, God protected me. He truly had a plan for my life. His careful, intentional plan doesn't just apply to me. The good news is that God has a plan for your life as well.

Searching for and discovering my birth family has taught me many things about myself. Together, we will explore those lessons within the chapters of this book. You will read my story along with the stories of other adoptees, adoptive parents, siblings, and more people who share about their lives with an adopted person.

Gratefulness is a common denominator in my story and the stories of other adoptees. You will recognize the central part God has played in all our lives.

As an adult, I have become more thankful over the years, realizing my birth mother chose not to abort me. Instead, she gave me life through adoption, and that opportunity provided me with a future full of dreams and possibilities.

Personal growth must also be listed as a benefit of my search. Some thirty-five years ago, I decided to sort through my adoption in counseling. This eventually led me to identify my own core values and beliefs. It was a precursor to gaining spiritual insight, which in turn led to more understanding and healing.

The result of this in my own life has been wholeness. Not perfection, just wholeness wrapped up with peace. Not just any peace; I'm talking about God's peace. Because His peace passes all understanding. It surrounds you, ensuring that no matter what you are facing, everything will be okay.

My trust in God began many years ago, and I can honestly say He has always cared for me. In this book, I will share key ways I've seen Him work and felt His presence.

Everyone's adoption journey is unique. There is no right or wrong way to take the steps to wholeness. Some adoptees struggle with mental health issues, and some do not. Some of us chose to search for our birth families, and some have no desire to do so. It is a very personal choice to decide to search for your birth family. Everyone's circumstances are different.

My hope as you read these pages is that you will be encouraged and also that as we examine our adoption stories together, you will learn to understand and overcome common issues we face. I am praying that as you read these pages, the Holy Spirit will guide your heart and mind, bringing your needs to the surface.

Thank you for coming along as I share my personal adoption story and my journey to wholeness.

Jesus Was There at Your Birth

The Moment Everything Began

CLOSE YOUR EYES FOR A MOMENT. Take a deep breath. Now, imagine yourself at your very beginning—not as you are now, but as you were then. A newborn. Helpless. Completely dependent. In that hospital room, there were decisions being made that have shaped your entire life. Decisions you had no voice in.

What if I told you that in that same room, invisible to the doctors and nurses, unseen by your birth mother and unknown to your future adoptive parents, there was Another present? What if the God Who knits babies together in their mothers' wombs was standing watch over you in that moment of separation? What if your story didn't actually begin with abandonment, but with divine appointment?

For adoptees, it's complicated to imagine our birth stories. While other people celebrate their birthdays with simple joy, ours come with questions: Why was I given away? Was I unwanted? Was there something wrong with me? Did my birth mother hold me? Did she cry? Did she care?

Today, let's start at the real beginning. We may have questions about the circumstances, but there is truth that changes the narrative of what happened in that moment you entered the world. The fact is that you were not alone. You have never been alone. And your life, from its very first breath, has been held in hands that will never let you go.

My Journey: God in the Delivery Room

Mease Hospital, Dunedin, Florida

Maggie was lying on the bed in the labor and delivery room as the nurses prepared for her to deliver. I wonder what thoughts and feelings swirled through her mind. Giving birth wasn't a new experience. She already had four children, who all shared the same father. Maggie obviously knew what to expect from childbirth. She had also previously placed her fifth child for adoption. I would be her sixth and the second that she would give away. Was this even a big deal for her?

Were her emotions twisted in a knot? Was she hoping once this birth was over that she could then move on with her life? What about the four children she had at home that had no idea a sibling was about to be born? Was she anxious? Did time pass slowly, waiting for the labor and delivery to finally be over?

Was she alone or was a family member with her? I wonder if Grace, her mother, was by her side? Shepard, the man she was involved with at the time of my birth, was he with her at the hospital? I know her younger sister Ardith wasn't there, because I've been told she was babysitting Robert and Ardith, the two oldest of Maggie's children. Tommy and Amber, the other two, were being watched by the Chapmans, their next-door neighbors.

Adoption Arrangements

Prior to my birth, all the adoption arrangements with the attorney had been finalized. Legal papers had been signed, and the adoptive parents were waiting to be notified of my birth. Even though Maggie knew she couldn't care for more children, I wonder if she had any second thoughts about giving me up. She carried me for nine months; did she form any attachment at all? Was she feeling any regrets or sadness?

Labor progressed, and the time came for delivery. The doctor and nurses knew the circumstances, that the baby being born was being adopted. The staff had procedures they followed in situations like this. Once born, nurses took the babies immediately to the nursery, not allowing the mother to see the infant. Since she'd done it before, Maggie knew what to expect. What was the mood in that delivery room? Was it somber and sad or joyful as a new life was about to enter the world?

God's Presence

There was another presence in that delivery room. Not a physical person that could be seen by the doctor and nurses, but a spiritual presence. I believe God knew me from the very moment of my conception. Jeremiah 1:5 states, "Before I formed you in the womb I knew you, before you were born I set you apart." The circumstances surrounding my birth didn't matter, because my heavenly Father was with me. Jesus and His angels were there in that delivery room, ready to receive me.

Even if my birth mother had no joy at that special moment, God did, and He was holding me tenderly in His loving arms. He knew what my future would be. God has always protected me, and even though my birth mother chose to surrender me, He has never stopped loving and caring for me.

Maggie's decision to place me for adoption may have been

viewed by others as weak, but personally, I believe her decision was guided by God. It was His plan for my life. Maggie struggled with being a mother, and she didn't always do a good job of caring for the children she already had. She struggled with depression and met with a psychiatrist for years. My siblings who Maggie did raise experienced times of both physical and emotional abuse. I choose to believe that she knew her home situation wouldn't allow her to handle any more children. Finances were tight, and she didn't need another mouth to feed.

Adopted Parents

I don't know when Maggie left the hospital, but I wonder if she returned home feeling empty, or if she mainly experienced a sense of relief? I'm confident that my adopted parents, Rosemary and George, were anxiously waiting to be told I had been safely delivered, and that I was healthy. After the disappointment of several miscarriages, they were about to start their own family.

Imagine the excitement and joy they felt knowing they were finally going to realize their dream of becoming parents, the fun they had preparing and decorating the nursery, throwing baby showers, buying baby clothes and supplies, and notifying family, friends, and coworkers. Emotions must have been overflowing as they waited for the day they would pick me up at the hospital. Like most new parents, they likely felt a mixture of happiness and fear.

Two days after I was born, George and Rosemary picked me up from Mease Hospital in Dunedin and took me to their home on Calumet Street in Clearwater, Florida. Their middle-class neighborhood was filled with families enjoying life in the fifties. Rosemary loved the play *Cyrano de Bergerac*, so she named me after Roxanne, the heroine of the play.

A New Love

Recently I discovered an old photo of my mom holding me the day I came home from the hospital. There was a handwritten note on the album page from George, my father. He wrote, "I wanted the chance to write this. My love and her new love. It won't replace or displace, it's just a new love. 3 days old just arriving home."

This began my journey as an adopted child, chosen by loving parents who desperately longed to have children. Perhaps you too were adopted into a loving home, but my goal by sharing is that you will recognize that no matter what the first days of your life looked like, God was near and has always had a plan for you.

We all desire to better understand ourselves, and part of that process, I believe, is to recognize the significant part God has played in our adoptions.

~

Barbara: When Birth Stories Get Complicated

Imagine growing up believing you'd been adopted by your step-father only to discover, after your mother's death, that you never were.

Barbara's life began with uncertainty. Her birth mother, Pauline, and her birth father, Cyril, were not married. It's likely that Cyril never even knew Pauline was pregnant. Barbara suspects her mother considered ending her pregnancy, but her strong, no-nonsense Seventh Day Adventist grandmother, Sallie, made it clear: That would not happen. Immediately after giving birth, Pauline left the newborn in Sallie's care, and she is the one who raised Barbara.

Barbara's memories of her mother are few. The only one

from childhood is a visit when Barbara was seven. Pauline had come to North Carolina, but she was sick the whole time and stayed in her bedroom. When Barbara was ten, her mother married a Colonel in the military, and soon after, the couple moved briefly to Japan.

At thirteen, Barbara left her grandmother's home for the first time to live with her mother and the Colonel in Virginia. They stayed there for about a year and a half. Pauline told her that the Colonel had adopted her so she could receive military benefits. At fifteen, the family moved to Germany, where Barbara graduated from high school before returning to the U.S. at seventeen. Over the years, Barbara came to feel that her mother was jealous of her close relationship with her stepfather.

Barbara married young. Her first husband, Harold, was the father of her three children: one infant daughter who died shortly after birth and two living children, Dirk and Vanna. Her second marriage was to James, and her third to Felix, a local businessman. Blending families with Felix brought five teenagers under one roof—and all the challenges that came with it.

In 1993, Barbara was preparing to marry her fourth husband, Gary, when she phoned her mother to share the news. The call left her stunned. Pauline answered, then asked, "Who is this?" When Barbara told her, "I'm your daughter," Pauline replied, "I don't have a daughter."

That moment forced Barbara to face the ache she had carried for years. After three years of counseling, she realized she had been searching for the father-love she never had. Seeking validation from men had led to her four marriages. She admits she learned to be deeply untrusting.

As she grew older and needed more care, Pauline returned to North Carolina to be near her sister, Peggy. At the end of her life, Pauline became ill, and Barbara cared for her during a two-week hospital stay. Not long after this, an injury led to sepsis, and Pauline passed away.

It was only while sorting through her mother's papers that Barbara discovered the truth: she had never been legally adopted by her stepfather, the Colonel. Her last name had simply been changed. The revelation left her feeling deeply deceived.

Barbara still wonders if her birth father ever knew about her. Cyril married six months after she was born and later had three children. From what those children have said, she believes that if he had known, he might have tried to be part of her life.

Tom & Ellen: When God Turns Rejection into Blessing

In their late twenties, Tom and Ellen began to talk seriously about adoption. Unable to conceive, and mindful of Tom's own family story—his brother had been born with epilepsy and cerebral palsy—they began to consider adoption. They thought surely there were healthy babies out there who needed parents. They applied to be adoptive parents through the Florida Department of Children and Families. Adoption was not an inexpensive option, as the adoption fee was $4,000, with half due once they were approved.

By March of 1987, Tom and Ellen had their approval in hand. Friends knew they were hoping to adopt, including Ellen's hairdresser, who happened to also style the hair of an attorney's wife. The attorney specialized in adoptions, and as it happened, he had two couples lined up to adopt a baby expected to be a girl—confirmed by three ultrasounds.

When the baby was born in May, however, it was a boy. The attorney called both couples, but neither wanted to proceed. That's when his wife remembered the couple her hairdresser had mentioned—Tom and Ellen. She called Ellen immediately.

Back at the hospital, the attorney discovered another "coincidence": one of the nurses caring for the newborn knew Tom and Ellen personally. The connections felt like confirmation. Tom and Ellen didn't hesitate—they said yes to the little boy.

There was one complication. When Tom called the Department of Children and Families to let them know they were adopting through an attorney, the woman handling their file was furious. The $2,000 deposit had never been collected, and she refused to release the letters of recommendation in their file. Realizing they needed to move forward on their own, Tom and Ellen began the process for a private adoption.

Even though they moved quickly to provide the legal requirements, the process took two weeks. During that time, the newborn boy stayed at the attorney's home. When it was finally time to bring the little baby home, Tom and Ellen had an opportunity to be an encouragement for adoption, as another expectant mother was at the home to observe the process. She was considering adoption for her own child and eagerly listened to Tom and Ellen's thoughts and experiences. Although Tom and Ellen don't know the choices that woman made, they hope she saw how adoption offers the opportunity for hope in a difficult situation.

Tom and Ellen named their son James, and he now goes by Jim. His birth mother had written two letters that she gave to Tom and Ellen. One was for them and the other for Jim to read when he was older. Tragically, the letter for Jim was lost decades later when their home was destroyed by a hurricane in 2022.

Tom had hoped his son would share his love for sports, but Jim's interests took a different path. Even at a very young age, he devoured books, reading Moby Dick long before most children his age could have tackled it. Later, he was diagnosed with ADHD, but with Ellen's training as a teacher, she knew how to support him through the challenges.

When Jim was around six or seven years old, Tom and Ellen

told him that he was adopted. A few years later, at twelve, he asked them not to share that fact with others.

Today, Jim is thirty-eight. He has encountered his share of adult struggles—battling weight and blood pressure issues, navigating a divorce, managing depression with the help of a mental health professional, and trying to find his footing financially.

What began with two families saying "no" became Tom and Ellen's greatest "yes." Their story is stitched together by conversations with a hairdresser, unexpected phone calls, and the unmistakable hand of God.

Your Journey: Reclaiming Your Beginning

We've just walked through a few stories of others' adoptions together. These stories may have landed with relief, or resistance, or maybe both at the same time. That's okay.

Let's take a step into making this personal by connecting with God as you consider your own story.

Reflection Moment

- How have you told your birth story to yourself? Take some time to write out an account of your entry into this world as though God is telling it. Imagine the scene when you entered this world. Think beyond the hospital staff or relatives in the room. Picture the God who formed you, standing over you with joy in His eyes. What might He have been whispering over your tiny frame? Imagine His presence in your earliest moments. What did He see? What did His heart feel?

- What do you think when you consider the possibility that your birth was planned? Let yourself imagine that you were not an accident. How would your heart shift if you believed that fully?
- What still hurts when you think about your beginning? Are there feelings of rejection? Abandonment? Feeling like you were "less than"? Write down the emotions you feel and give yourself time and permission to look at each word and experience the fullness of those feelings.
- God Himself uses the language of adoption to describe His relationship with all of His children. Consider this encouraging verse: "The Spirit you received does not make you slaves, so that you live in fear again; rather, the Spirit you received brought about your adoption to sonship. And by him we cry, 'Abba Father'" (Romans 8:15).

What does God's adoption of His children say about your value? How would your life look different if you fully embraced the deep love God has for you, His adopted child?

Significant Next Steps

Some reading this book know who your birth parents are. You may even have a relationship with them. Others of you do not know. Maybe you've searched before and didn't find answers. Or maybe you have not been ready to take that step yet. Opening the door into your birth family is a personal decision, not to be rushed or pressured into.

If you are ready to explore unknowns of the past, I suggest speaking first with your adoptive parents. They may have more information and be able to share the experience they had when they first met you and any details from those early moments with you. From there, pray about next steps. If you do choose to learn more about your birth family, tell others your plans. You'll want support from loving people in your life as you uncover the past.

Prayer

Creator God,

You were there. In that hospital room, in my first breath—You were there. When my birth mother released me, You caught me. When tears were shed, You collected them. When decisions were made that would forever change my life, You were orchestrating a plan.

Heal the wounds I carry from my beginning. Where I have believed I was unwanted, show me I was chosen. Where I have felt abandoned, reveal Your constant presence. Where I have seen only loss, help me also see Your loving provision.

Thank You for my birth mother, who gave me life. Whether by choice or circumstance, she carried me and delivered me into this world. Bless her, wherever she is.

Thank You for my adoptive parents, who gave me a home. In their longing for a child, You saw their hearts and chose them for me.

Thank You that my story didn't begin with human plans but with Your divine purpose. I am fearfully and wonderfully made. My days were written in Your book. My life is not an accident.

Help me to live from this truth, to build my identity on the foundation of being twice chosen—once by earthly parents and eternally by You.

In the name of Jesus, who was also adopted by an earthly father,

Amen.

A Final Thought

Your birth story may be complicated. It may include pain, loss, addiction, poverty, violence, or simply inconvenient timing. But none of that changes this truth: In that delivery room, whether anyone realized it or not, the God of the universe was present, watching over a baby He had been planning since before time began.

You were not alone then. You are not alone now. And every breath you take is proof that God had a purpose for your life that no human decision could thwart.

Your story didn't begin with abandonment. It began with divine appointment. And the God who was faithful to bring you through that first day will be faithful to complete the good work He began in you.

God's Protection Through It All

MANY PEOPLE DON'T UNDERSTAND that it is a gift to feel safe. For many of us who have been adopted, we don't take safety for granted. Think of who your "safe person" was as a child. Maybe you didn't have a consistent person or the feeling was fleeting, but somewhere in your story, God placed a protector. Maybe you had a teacher who saw something special in you. A neighbor who always had cookies and a kind word if you stopped by. Perhaps you had a grandparent whose lap was a refuge.

For adoptees, these protectors often stand between us and a world that doesn't necessarily understand our unique struggles. They become God's hands and feet, His provision for children who have already experienced the trauma of separation, even if we don't remember it.

Sometimes protection comes through people who love us. Sometimes it comes through circumstances that remove us from danger. And sometimes—though it's hard to see at the time—protection comes disguised as pain that redirects our path.

When we get down to analyzing our past, it often feels like it's the negative memories we're encouraged to concentrate on. Even though it's not healthy to repress the painful memories, I encourage you to also recall the good memories, times you felt cared for and loved, safe and secure.

My Journey: The People God Placed in My Path

Influential People

I am grateful for the people God strategically placed in my life, loving and caring people that crossed my path, made me feel safe, and impacted my circumstances. My mother and father divorced when I was three or four years old. That's another reason it became even more important for me to rely on not only my mother but others nearby for the feelings of security we all deeply crave. Not all my memories are good; there are some that are not. But all these experiences have shaped me into the person I have become.

Frank and Anna

Frank and Anna immediately come to mind when I think about influential people from my childhood. They were my godparents and a stable influence, and my life was shaped by them. Frank and Anna were like family to me. They had four children, and their youngest daughter, Debbie, was my best friend. They attended the Episcopal Church each Sunday, and at some point, my mom decided I should attend church with them. She would drop me off at their house and I would eat breakfast with them, and then off we would go to Sunday School and Church.

Frank was a surgeon, and Anna was a stay-at-home mom. Their large, spacious home was in an upper-middle-class neighborhood called Harbor Bluffs. Even though they weren't blood relatives, I called them Aunt and Uncle. Uncle Frank had a wicked, dry sense of humor, likely inherited from his British relatives. He and my mom always enjoyed discussing the political issues of the day and solving the world's problems. Aunt Anna was warm, loving, and had a close, special friendship with my mom.

I fondly remember the boat rides and scalloping we did together. They played a big part in my young life until we moved away for a brief time when I was in the 5th grade. Even when we didn't live near them, they always stayed in touch. I still have a treasured Christmas stocking my aunt knitted for me as a child, with Santa Claus on the front and my name on the top. I proudly hang it every year at Christmas, and it reminds me of my aunt's love.

James and May

Even though my maternal grandparents, James and May, didn't live close, they were still involved in my life. They resided in a small white wood-frame house, with a sprawling oak tree that shaded the entire front yard. In the summer, my mom would put me on a Greyhound bus in Largo and send me to my grandparents in Fort Meade to visit for a week or two. The town was so small that there wasn't a bus depot, so it stopped at the Orange Blossom Café for passengers to get on and off. Grandpa would be there waiting for me when the bus arrived.

Summers in Fort Meade were magical. I swung on the wooden porch swing while reading books and picked vegetables in the garden. If grandma needed groceries, she sent me to the A&P with a blank check she had signed and the list. The cashier knew my grandma and would fill in the check for me. Those were different times. We also never locked our doors, often left our keys in the car, and joined our neighbors in taking care of one another.

I still have a special, faded photo on my dresser of me sitting on grandpa's lap, with my long legs hanging down. His sweet smile could light up any room, and he was always warm, loving, and gave me lots of hugs. After he got home from work, we would watch television together in the living room. He made the best cheese toast for breakfast, baked under the broiler until the cheese puffed up. We often went to town together to run errands. He was a gentle man, kind to everyone he met. Everyone loved him, especially me, and he was one of the few positive male role models in my life.

Grandma had three children. The oldest was a son, the middle child a daughter, and my mother the youngest. At some point in her life, my grandmother became an alcoholic. I mean a bad alcoholic. Even though it was many years ago, I still remember her sitting in a green wooden rocker on the front porch sipping Busch beer. That daily routine lasted from eleven in the morning till eleven at night. She wouldn't sleep in a bedroom because she was claustrophobic and instead slept on a daybed in the corner of the living room. Besides beer, Salem cigarettes were her other vice.

Rosemary

The bond between a mother and her child is special and like no other. That includes both natural and adopted children. You may have heard the old saying, "You will never understand how much I love you until you have a child of your own." That maternal attachment is key to our development. I was so blessed to have Rosemary as my mother. Before I was born, she suffered through several miscarriages and longed to be a mother.

Her relationship with her own mother was not an easy one. For some reason, my grandmother treated my mom differently than her other two children, which I believe contributed to mom's insecurity. She was the first one in her family to graduate from high school, a beautiful blonde who enjoyed drawing and had such a beautiful voice that she sang with a group on the radio. She had a very tender heart and loved all kinds of animals.

As difficult as her relationship was with her mom, she always treated her with love and respect until the day she died. Thankfully, my grandfather provided my mom with lots of encouragement and love. I think this sweet man had to be somewhere on the Saint list for living with my alcoholic grandma and all the drama that went with that situation.

Moving to Lansing

Mom quit her job at Honeywell when I was in the fifth grade. She sold our house and followed a man she had met and thought she loved up to Lansing, Michigan. Leaving our home, friends, and family and moving across the country was not easy. I can only imagine the anxiety my mom must have experienced during that time. She needed to locate a place for us to live, enroll me in a new school, and find herself a job. Michigan was nothing at all like Florida; they had snow, something I had never seen before. Even though it was difficult, she accomplished everything that was needed to get us reestablished in a new city and state. A few months later, she was completely devastated to learn this man she'd uprooted her life for was leading a double life. Shockingly, it turned out he was married with children and had no intention of marrying my mother.

Suicide Attempt

Mom was totally broken when she realized she had left behind our life in Florida and moved us across the country to follow a man, a man she loved who was not who she thought he was. One night she locked herself in her bedroom and took pills to commit suicide. When I couldn't get her to come to the door or respond, I got scared. I went upstairs to get the couple who lived above us and asked for help. They somehow got the bedroom door open, and we found my mother unconscious. We called an ambulance to transport her to the hospital. I remember being so frightened, wondering what was going to happen to her. What would happen to me if she died? She was all I had.

Later I learned my mother had died at the hospital, but thankfully they were able to revive her. She was in a coma for a while, and they wouldn't allow me to visit. They did ask me to pack some things for mom, and her friend Elaine took them to the hospital. I packed a suitcase with her nightgown, toiletries, clothes, and her Bible.

The hospital sent back the suitcase with the Bible still inside. I suppose they didn't give her the Bible because she was in a psychiatric unit. I wasn't yet a Christian, but I knew that my mom's Bible was important to her, and that's why I sent it to the hospital. Often mental health professionals disregard faith as a part of the healing process. But Jesus is the Great Physician, and he still performs miracles today. Thankfully mom survived the suicide attempt and was eventually released from the hospital and started seeing a counselor.

God's Protection

I now know God was protecting me during this tough time. The love and support of family and friends comforted me, helping me deal with the trauma of my mom's attempt to take her life. I don't remember a lot about that situation, but even as a child, I was strong. I wonder how a child finds such strength at a young age. I can only speculate it was given supernaturally by God.

We all face difficulties in life where we may feel weak and uncertain. We ask if we can continue. The good news for everyone is that God loves us, and if we cry out to Him, He will answer our prayers and provide us with what we need to get through any situation.

When life throws a curve, sometimes you have to figure out a way to survive. There is no doubt in my mind that I'm a survivor because God brought people to help me get through tough times, not only as a child, but also as a teenager and even an adult. Mom's suicide attempt in Lansing was certainly not my last experience with hard times.

Second Suicide Attempt

After moving back to Florida, Mom tried to take her own life for the second time when I was in the sixth grade. She was again struggling with depression and loneliness. For an unknown reason, my mother stopped her counseling visits and was trying to navigate life on her own as a single mom. Many years later, she confessed her reason for attempting suicide was her fear of having to raise a teenager alone.

On her second attempt, she had once again locked herself in her bedroom, telling me she was going to listen to music and not to bother her. When quite some time had passed and she wouldn't answer the door, I got worried and went and got our next-door neighbor. He had to break a window to get into her room and found her unconscious again. The neighbor and I followed the ambulance to the hospital.

He waited with me for a while but eventually went home, leaving me in the lobby of the hospital. I was twelve years old, and I clearly remember the receptionist telling me I couldn't stay there. I informed her in my most adult voice that I most certainly was staying there, because my mom was there! Thankfully my mother's close friend Paul, who had been planning to visit our house that night, came to my rescue. When he arrived at our home and discovered we were gone, he went to the neighbor's house, who told him what happened and where to find us. Paul found me at the hospital and took me home.

I remember being so frightened that night, wondering once

more if my mom might die. If she died, who would take care of me? Where would I live? All I knew was that I needed my mom. Praying, I pleaded and asked God to please not let my mommy die. I was worried and felt so alone. God heard the innocent prayer of a child who was desperately pleading for Him to save her mom. Thankfully she survived and came home and started seeing a counselor again. I finished sixth grade, and we moved into a mobile home in a park located near her job.

Discerning God

As a seventy-one-year-old, I have had years of opportunity to reflect on my life and notice how God's hand has always guided and protected me. When I searched for and found my birth family and uncovered details of my adoption, I began to view my adoption in a whole new light. The discovery experience transformed and settled me. My perspective changed. I will admit it took hard work to sort through some of the emotional baggage, but I say this as encouragement that this journey to understanding our origin story is full of valuable self-discovery.

Wherever you are in the understanding of your adoption, I'd like to encourage you to consider: What would happen if you believed that God has had a direct hand in your life? That it wasn't by chance that you ended up with your adopted family? God chose that family for you. Don't feel guilty if you wish you had ended up with a different family, because not every adoptee had a loving and supportive family. But there may have been a reason you ended up with them.

Shared Experiences: Others' Stories of Protection

Carol: When God Provides the Perfect Timing

Carol and I became friends in a therapeutic yoga class. At some point, a conversation revealed she too was adopted. Born in 1947 and given up at birth, the first adoptive family that took her home from the hospital returned her, saying she cried too much! A second family took her, and unbelievably, they also returned her for crying too much! So, at four days old, she was sent to a children's home.

Based on this traumatic start, it might not seem like it, but God had big plans for Carol. He had already selected the perfect family for her: adoptive parents who were farmers in Missouri and wanted a child so much. Back in the forties, the children's home had a long list of requirements for adoptive parents. Some things on the list we probably can't relate to today. The prospective parents needed to have $5,000 in the bank, sponsors, indoor plumbing, a telephone, electricity, and the family had to be the *same religion as the baby!* There were also age limits that didn't allow adoptive parents to be over forty years old.

That's where Carol's future parents ran into a problem. They met all the requirements, except that the father was forty-four years old. The orphanage agreed to waive the age limit standard if the couple took Carol, the child who kept being returned. At this point, Carol was almost a year old. Because she had been kept in a playpen for most of her life, she didn't know how to walk. Once she went with her new parents back to their Missouri home, she started walking in just one week. Her adoption was finalized one week before her first birthday.

Carol shared that growing up as an only child, she never felt like she really fit in with her adopted family. When she turned seventy, a close friend helped her search and find her birth family. She learned that her birth mother was twenty-six years old and unmarried when she had given birth to Carol and that she had died when Carol was only sixteen years old. Although Carol never learned who her father was, the search revealed that she had two younger half brothers, Bob and Paul, who shared the same father.

The search not only led to Carol being connected with her brothers but also helped them to become reconnected with extended family. That same year of her discovery, Carol drove to Missouri with her brother Bob to attend a large family reunion. The reunion also allowed her brother the opportunity to reconnect with his larger family, and he has stayed connected with them regularly as well.

As Carol pieced together more information about her birth family, she learned that by being adopted, she had been removed from a horrible situation with her birth mother. God had protected her. Bob shared that their mother had lived with an alcoholic for many years, which had created a very difficult and dysfunctional environment for Bob and Paul.

While growing up, Carol regularly attended the United Church of Christ with her adoptive parents. They were parents who prayed with her daily, and she always felt God's presence in her life. Now, at the age of seventy-eight, she says, "I am constantly amazed at the miracles that God performs. I wonder how anyone could possibly doubt his existence." Her parents taught her that if something happens to you, you just decide to make a plan to get through it with the grace of God.

Kristen: Protected Even in Foster Care

Kristen is a close friend of my stepdaughter Michelle, and their families spend a lot of time together. Kristen was born in 1989 in Lynchburg, Virginia and spent the first six weeks of her life in foster care. She was placed for adoption by an agency called Liberty Godparent Home. Her adoptive parents were from southern Indiana, where her dad served as a Baptist pastor and her mom worked as a teacher.

Kristen was the first of two adopted girls, followed by her younger sister, Kaitlin. The family openly discussed that the girls were adopted. She and Kaitlin were opposites, with her being a tomboy and Kristen being girly. Their mom homeschooled her girls, and Kristen describes her childhood as busy, with an active social life. Because her dad was so busy as a pastor, she is closer to her mom than to her dad.

In the ninth grade, her family moved to Lakeland from Jacksonville, Florida. At the age of sixteen, Kristen asked her mom if she could contact the adoption agency for information on her birth parents. Both she and her mom wrote letters, and Liberty forwarded them to her birth mother.

Her birth mom, Kathryn, responded immediately with a box full of letters, photos, gifts, and teddy bears she had collected over the years. When Kristen turned eighteen, and while attending college, she again contacted Liberty, requesting her birth mother's contact information. She received an email with the information, and she immediately called her.

Kathryn invited Kristen to visit her in Virginia. It was an emotional departure when her mom and sister dropped her off at the airport for the trip. Upon arriving, Kristen immediately saw that she had inherited her tall height from her birth mom. She was warmly received by her mom and her mom's extended family. That began a renewed relationship, and Kristen now calls her adoptive parents Mom and Dad and calls her birth mom by her given name of Kathryn.

Since the age of eighteen, Kristen had been told her birth father, Armando, was dead. She decided in November of 2022 to set up an international Ancestry.com account to search for his family. Through that decision, she discovered a total of twelve aunts and uncles, as well as Armando's death certificate.

In December of the same year, Kristen and her husband Josh flew to Mexico to meet her birth father's extensive family. While there, she learned that her father had planned to marry Kathryn, but while traveling back to Mexico to retrieve an engagement ring, he was killed in an auto accident, solving the mystery of why he hadn't returned to marry Kathryn.

Kristen believes that God played a huge part in her adoption. She thinks there was a possibility Kathryn might have aborted her, but thankfully she instead chose to place her for adoption. She believes that God led her family to Lakeland, Florida, because years later, that is where she met her future husband. They now have three beautiful children.

As for her thoughts in general about adoption, Kristen doesn't believe adoption is for everyone and doesn't feel like our country adequately supports adoption. For many seeking to adopt, the cost is a deterrent. For example, she knows of a couple who paid $40,000 to adopt a child five years ago here in the United States. There are many challenges associated with adoption, and this high cost is a major one prohibiting loving families from making this choice to expand their family.

Diane: Protected by Love

Diane and I attended the same Bible study at our former church. Over time I learned that like me, she was adopted. Born in 1948 in New Orleans, Diane was placed for adoption through the St. Vincent de Paul Orphanage. Her birth mom had been eighteen years old, and she went to the same gynecologist as Diane's future adoptive mom. The doctor played matchmaker, and the rest is history.

Diane was told that at five days old, she went home with her new family. Oddly, there are no photos of her until the age of four months, so she suspects she may have stayed longer in the orphanage than she was told.

One year after Diane was placed with her adoptive parents, they returned to court to finalize the adoption. The name of the judge on the legal documents was Judge Blessing, which her mother said was a sign that God's hand was in the adoption. Before the adoption, her mom had lost a baby, whom she had carried full term. After this loss, she had four miscarriages. Surprisingly, after adopting Diane, her mom gave birth to three more children. Diane looked different from her siblings, because she was small in stature, and her siblings were tall and large.

Diane's childhood was very happy. Her family loved and accepted her fully, and she was close to her siblings. In addition, her two sets of grandparents showered her with attention. Even though she always knew she was adopted, no one ever really talked about her adoption.

When she was very young, her parents had given her the book *The Chosen Baby* by Valentina Pavlovna Wasson to help explain her adoption. Believing that her dad would be hurt if Diane tried to locate her birth family, Diane's mother waited until he had passed to help her search for them. They hired a private investigator, but he was unable to find any information.

Around 2010 or 2011, Diane located an obituary of her birth mother and discovered she had been an organist at a Baptist church in Pensacola, Florida. The obituary stated her mom had no children. But after she contacted the pastor of the church, he sent Diane a photo of her mom, and she was able to locate a cousin using Ancestry.com. She was hoping the cousin would help her with family health information, but she wouldn't respond. Ten years ago, Diane's daughter called the same cousin, and sadly, she still wouldn't provide any information. Diane was never able to identify her birth father.

Like many of the adoptees I spoke with, Diane believes that God had a plan for her life from the moment of her conception.

She is grateful that her adoption was never hidden and believes adoptive parents should be open about the adoption as the child grows up, answering the child's questions as best they can.

Going Deeper: Understanding God's Protection in Adoption

The Theology of Protection

A common theme I discovered when interviewing adoptees is the belief that God used adoption as a grace to protect them. Whether that means He protected them from being aborted or from an abusive childhood, or from an unknown life of potential difficulty, through the gift of adoption, God changed the circumstances of their early years and the trajectory of their lives.

What I want to clarify in this focus on God's protection through adoption is that I'm not suggesting adopted children are somehow more special or more protected than biological children. That's not it at all. Rather, this is a recognition that in the midst of what begins as profound loss—that primal separation from birth parents—God often provides unexpected forms of protection and care. He takes what was broken and builds something beautiful, even through the pain.

We can see throughout history that God has always used adoption as a means of graceful protection. The Bible overflows with stories of God's protection for the vulnerable. James 1:27 pierces straight to the heart: "Religion that God our Father accepts as pure and faultless is this: to look after orphans and widows in their distress." Throughout Scripture, we see God's fierce love for those who are alone, displaced, or without family. He calls Himself "Father to the fatherless." That's not just a nice phrase—it's a promise, a declaration of His character.

In Genesis, baby Moses was saved from Pharaoh's decree to kill baby Israelite boys by being hidden in a basket, protected by river reeds until the princess found him and decided to raise him as her own. Moses went on to be God's chosen leader to free His people from slavery in Egypt and settle them in a new land.

Queen Esther too was an orphan, raised by her cousin and placed in the right time and place to save her people from being destroyed. Even Jesus as a child was protected through Joseph's adoption of Him, a child not his own.

God has always worked through adoption.

Types of Protection in Adoption Stories

As I've thought about these stories I've collected—Diane's, Carol's, Ellen's, and dozens more—I've noticed patterns in how God protects. Let me show you what I mean:

Physical Protection: Many adoptees discover they were removed from situations that could have destroyed them—abuse, neglect, addiction, violence. I think of my own birth mother, struggling with mental illness and poverty. While not all birth parents face these challenges (and we must be careful not to paint them all with the same brush), when they do, adoption can literally be life-saving. This also applies to the adoptive families God places us into. I often think about my mother's suicide attempt when I was eleven. What if I had not been with her? What if we did not have family or friends to help us through that difficult time?

Emotional Protection: Here's something people don't always understand: adoptive parents invest an enormous level of emotional energy into their adoptive children, often long before the children ever enter their home. There are many reasons why people choose to adopt. Sometimes they adopt because of genuine concern and love for children who need care. Sometimes adoption stories start with a couple who aren't able to have children on their own. Often it's a mixture of these and other emotional scenarios. Adoption usually begins with intentional love, and that creates deep security. Adoptive parents fight many battles for their children and sometimes spend their life savings to bring a child home. That kind of wanting creates a unique form of protection. Diane's parents, after five lost babies, knew exactly how precious a newborn baby is. That knowledge and the emotional investment secured their attachment to her as with any biological parents.

Spiritual Protection: Many adoptees are placed in families where they learn about God's love. Being raised with this spiritual understanding might not have happened in their birth families and demonstrates how God goes to great lengths to make Himself known and bring people to Himself. That even includes moving tiny newborn babies into situations where they will grow up learning about His love and grace.

Providential Protection: These are the "coincidences" that make you catch your breath—like Carol's parents being just a few years over the age limit but getting approved anyway, or Jim's nurse knowing his adoptive parents, or Diane's adoption being finalized by Judge Blessing. When you see enough of these "coincidences," you start to realize they're not coincidences at all, but evidence of God's fingerprints all over our stories. On a regular basis, God is intervening into our stories to protect and guide our way.

Recognizing Protection Doesn't Mean Denying Pain

Even though I'm highlighting the ways God protects people through adoption, I don't want to be misunderstood. Embracing God's protection through adoption does not minimize the loss of your birth family. It doesn't mean pretending adoption is always easy or ignoring the real trauma of separation. I have talked to many adoptees and understand that while there are so many "good" adoptions, there are also "bad" adoptions. God's protection may coexist with legitimate pain. They're not mutually exclusive circumstances.

In fact, I live with reconciling this tension every day. While I remember and am grateful for the provision of my adoptive parents and of my godparents, Frank and Anna, it also brings me heartache to think about my birth mother's mental illness. Then there was the bittersweet experience of being reunited with my birth family. All of these providential and painful realities coexist in the same story—my story. Your story too, I imagine.

Your Journey: Recognizing God's Protection

How do you reconcile the tension between God's protection and the reality of painful circumstances that may have existed at your beginning? Perhaps you haven't permitted yourself to think through these complex emotions in the past. If you're ready, the answers below will serve as a guide to recognizing God's hand in the circumstances of your life.

Reflection Moment

1. Who were the "Franks and Annas" in your life? These would be people who steadied your world, even when the details of your life felt chaotic.
2. When in your growing-up years did God's protection come disguised as pain?
3. What might life have been like for you if you hadn't been adopted?
4. Where do you still need God's protection today?

5. How can your story of protection multiply as protection for someone else?

Significant Next Steps

- Reflect on the "protectors" in your life. If you're a visual thinker, map out your relationships. Draw yourself at the center. Around you, write down every person who helped to make you feel safe.
- Next, pick one or more of these people who showed they care. Write a letter to thank that person. Tell them what it meant.
- Pass the role of protector on. Do you know a child or teenager who needs stability? What are practical ways that you could show up for them and change their world?
- Our bodies carry the anxiety and tension of being on alert. Pause in a quiet moment and think about the circumstances of a moment when you felt completely safe. Let your body lean into this peaceful feeling and relax knowing that God is your protector who makes this feeling of security possible throughout the stressful circumstances of our lives.

Prayer

Protective Father,

Thank You for being my shield and defender, even when I didn't know You were there. Thank You for the people You placed in my path—the ones who stood between me and harm, who offered love when I felt unloved, who saw potential when I felt worthless.

Help me to see Your protection even in the painful parts of my story. Where I see only loss, show me Your preservation. Where I see only rejection, show me Your redirection. Where I see only abandonment, show me Your adoption into Your eternal family.

For the protectors I've forgotten, remind me. For the protectors I've taken for granted, humble me. For the protection I still need, provide. For the protection I can offer others, equip me.

Make me a protector for others, as You have protected me.

In the name of Jesus, who protects us eternally,

Amen.

A Final Thought

Protection in adoption isn't about having an experience that looks like a picture-perfect story. Carol was returned twice before finding her family. My mother attempted suicide when I was young.

Kristen spent six weeks in foster care. Diane will never know her birth father's name. Yet in each story—broken and beautiful—God's protective hand is visible.

God has protected you as well. The details of realizing what you were protected from might be hidden under layers of pain so thick you can't imagine digging through them. Perhaps you were protected by unexpected people you've never thought to thank. Your story of God's protection might look completely different than you wished, but He never for a moment stopped caring for you.

The question isn't whether God protected you; it's whether you're ready to sort through these circumstances. I encourage you to take the next step to reconcile in your mind the outstanding questions and emotions you may not have yet addressed. Once you do, everything changes. Not because the pain disappears, but because you realize you were never as abandoned as you believed. You were held, even in moments of separation. You were loved, at every single moment.

That's the mystery and the miracle of adoption: In our stories of loss, God is especially near. When we imagine abandonment, God tells us we are chosen. Our challenge is to look for the ways God has never left us alone.

Sometimes, we need each other to lean on as we face the hard questions.

Chosen Twice

I HAVE OFTEN WONDERED why some adoptees seem drawn to faith while others run from it. There's something about being adopted once, at birth, that makes us uniquely sensitive to the idea of being adopted again. If we make the decision to enter a relationship with God, it is true that we are adopted a second time. It is my belief that this second adoption is even better than the first. This time, it's not about meeting someone's need for a child, but it's about a God who wants you simply because He loves you.

For some of us, faith feels like coming home. Finally, we belong somewhere unquestionably. Even if our earthly adoption papers are sealed, our salvation is an open book. No one can question whether we really belong in God's family.

For others, faith feels dangerous. We've already been rejected once—what if God changes His mind and rejects us too? What if we're not good enough for Him to keep? What if this Father also decides we're too much trouble?

Even if we embrace a life of faith, church itself becomes

complicated. We can never predict when there will be a sermon about God as Father, which pulls up those emotions where the wounds from our earthly fathers run deep. Then there's the talk about being "born again," when our first birth led to relinquishment. There's regular use at church of metaphors about adoption into God's family. These thoughts can distract us as we begin thinking about our earthly adoption, which carries so much complexity.

But what if spiritual adoption could actually heal the wounds of earthly adoption? What if being chosen by God could reframe being chosen by adoptive parents? What if the unconditional love we always craved is actually available, from a God who never will fail us?

Let me tell you about the night I discovered I wasn't just adopted once, but twice, and how that second adoption changed my perspective entirely.

My Journey: The Night Everything Changed

Junior High: Searching Without Knowing It

That first day of junior high school stays with me. Standing in the hot Florida sun in my ugly plaid Sears chubbette dress, I felt dizzy. The teacher noticed that I looked pale, like I might pass out, and told me to bend over so blood would go to my head. Looking back, I was off-balance in more ways than one. I was searching for something but didn't know what.

As the year progressed, we settled into a routine where Mom drove me to school each morning. After school, I'd walk to Publix and wait on the little bench inside, where it was cool. I'd sit there watching people while Mom finished work at the engineering company. I felt like I was always waiting—waiting for something to happen, waiting for something I didn't even know yet that I was missing.

My favorite classes were the electives. Mrs. Welch taught home economics: cooking, sewing, all the skills assumed needed for making a home. I loved learning these skills, though I couldn't say why they mattered so much to me. In Mr. Thomas's art class, I often lost myself in painting and drawing. Art let me express things I had no words for. It was like praying before I knew what prayer was.

St. David's Church

In eighth grade, God used my mother's coworkers to draw me to Himself. When Mom found out her coworkers went to St. David's Episcopal Church, she asked if I could go with them on Sundays. They agreed, and that was when I began to see God working in my life, even though He had been near me since before I was born.

My years at St. David's were happy and fulfilling. There were plenty of adults who guided me in my spiritual life. I joined the choir in ninth grade, attended a youth group, served as an acolyte, and did volunteer work. My high school years were a wonderful, positive experience, and my involvement at St. David's played a big part in that.

The youth group became my second family. We met on Sunday nights at the church, sitting on the floor, eating pizza, and talking about everything—school, parents, dating, and God. Our youth leaders, Yvonne and Bill, who were only about twelve years older than us, seemed so wise. They had a way of making the Bible feel relevant to our teenage lives.

I remember one night they asked us, "How many of you sometimes feel like you don't really belong anywhere?" Almost every hand went up. Then Bill said, "That feeling of not belonging? That's your heart telling you that you were made for another world. You were made for God's kingdom." My feeling of being different made sense.

Dave

Also when I was in eighth grade, Mom met Dave at work, and they started dating. He had a son who shared his name, and we decided to call him Little Dave. The four of us would go to the beach, the drive-in movies, have picnics in the park, and we shared lots of fun times. Dave proposed and he and mom married in April, just a few months after they started dating. Suddenly there were four of us living in our two-bedroom mobile home. My new stepbrother had to sleep on the couch. Not long after they married, Little Dave ended up moving back to New Jersey to live with his mother.

For me, it was a big change having a father around for the first time that I could remember. We all had to adjust. One of the adjustments for me and Dave was making sure I had a ride to and from my activities until I was old enough to get my driver's license. One of the places I regularly needed rides to and from was church for services and activities. I distinctly remember my dad complaining about having to drive me to church, asking Mom if I had to be there every time the doors were open! What parent complains about their child going to church too much?

Free Fare

Another significant turning point in my life happened when I was in the tenth grade. We had a special assembly at our high school for a performing singing group called Free Fare. They came from St. Pete and sang Christian pop music at that school day assembly. Everyone was invited to come back that night to hear their full concert. My best friend Becky and I decided to go. That concert changed my life forever.

I remember exactly what I was wearing: a navy-blue jumper with a white turtleneck and a red scarf. High school students packed the gymnasium and created an atmosphere filled with electric energy. Free Fare wasn't like any Christian group I'd heard before. They played real music—the kind we actually listened to on the radio—but with lyrics about love and hope and purpose.

After the group sang their last song, the band members presented the gospel. They talked about having a personal relationship with Jesus. I'd never heard about that at my traditional Episcopal church. They told us if we wanted to accept Jesus as our Savior to tear off the corner of our concert ticket. Both Becky and I tore our corners off.

Before we left, the group announced a drawing to win one of their albums. To enter the contest, we simply needed to write our name on our ticket and drop it into the box. When they prepared to draw the ticket, I remember standing there thinking, "God, I don't even know if You're real, but if You are, could You just show me? Could You let me win that album so I know You hear me?" It was my sincere prayer, asking God to prove He was real. I know, that was shallow of me, but hey, I was only sixteen years old. Sometimes, an honest cry is what God desires the most.

Well, guess what? I won the album! God answered the simple prayer of a brand-new Christian. When they called my name, I couldn't believe it. Becky started jumping up and down with me. It felt like God had just winked at me, saying, "Yes, I'm real. Yes, I hear you. And yes, you matter to Me."

Jesus Movement

Across the country in the 1970's, the Jesus Movement prompted a spiritual awakening. It began on the west coast and spread across North and Central America as well as Europe. In 1971, the story made the cover of Time Magazine, as young people were finding new life in Jesus. It impacted society, and I was part of that movement.

Many students in my high school were accepting Jesus as their Savior, and lives were being changed. We had a large non-denominational Bible study for teens that met weekly. Sometimes there would be fifty or sixty kids crammed into Bruce and Lorraine's living room, sitting on the floor, sharing testimonies and studying Scripture. This period in my life produced tremendous spiritual growth. I learned a boldness that allowed me to confidently pray for others, expecting results. I had wonderful, godly adults who guided me as I grew, and I was blessed by their love and encouragement. They were always willing to answer my many questions.

The Living Bible was the first modern translation I owned that made Scripture understandable. Most of us had grown up with the King James Version, but the Living Bible made Scripture come alive. I remember reading it under my covers with a flashlight after my parents thought I was asleep. I couldn't get enough. My circle of friends attended church retreats together, and we encouraged one another in our spiritual journeys. This was a time of much joy and happiness.

I was hungry for anything of God. I prayed, asking to be filled to overflowing with His precious Holy Spirit, and He did just that. One night at a prayer meeting, I felt something I'd never experienced before—like electricity running through my body, like being filled to overflowing with love. I didn't understand the power I was feeling, but instead of being frightened, I felt more at peace than I'd ever been in my life.

While all of this was going on in my life, I had questions about the Episcopal Church. My denomination was a liturgical denomination, with Holy Communion every Sunday and a lot of traditions. I remember asking my priest why the Episcopal Church wasn't more evangelical. I don't remember his answer, but in time, there were programs introduced like Faith Alive weekends, where team members shared their personal testimonies. This type of program was successful in introducing church members to a personal and intimate relationship with Jesus. The Jesus Movement had an impact on other denominations as well. It even resulted in the charismatic movement that began in 1967 in the Roman Catholic church.

Order of the Holy Family

In my senior year of high school, I learned about a religious order in Denver, Colorado that ministered to the homeless, drug addicts, alcoholics, and other street people in need. The Order of the Holy Family included both men and women who were dedicated to serving others in the name of Christ. My mom was less than pleased that her only child wanted to leave home at the age of eighteen and move to Colorado. She made it clear that she didn't agree with my idea of joining this religious order. My dad thought I should do what I wanted and at least give it a try.

I spent hours reading about monastic life, about people who gave up everything to serve God. Something appealed to me about belonging so completely to something bigger than myself. Maybe it was my adoption, always wondering where I belonged, that made me crave that kind of total commitment. I wanted to be "all in" somewhere, with someone, for something that mattered.

Looking back, I have the perspective of an older, and hopefully wiser, woman. I recognize my feelings and desires were natural for that age and life stage. When we are young, naïve, and spiritually immature, we think we can change the world. In reality, before that might possibly happen, we need to develop maturity and knowledge and gain some years of life experience to draw on. Even though this opportunity intrigued me, I became distracted by love and got engaged soon after graduation.

Graduation

When I graduated from high school in June of 1972, I was working part-time at a department store and not sure of what my future held. I had met a nice young man at a New Year's Eve party at the beginning of that year, and we had dated for a few months, but then stopped, and then started a few months later when he called again. We were still dating when I graduated, and then we married in December of 1972.

He came from a good family, and we had several things in common. We attended the same church, he was also adopted at birth, and I sang in the choir with his dad. He was polite, clean cut, and for all intents and purposes looked good on paper. However, sadly, he was not at all where I was spiritually. Even though we worshiped in the same denomination, our hearts were not in the same place.

Looking back, I can see that I was trying to fit into a life that looked right from the outside but didn't match who I was becoming on the inside. The Jesus Movement had changed me. I wasn't the same girl who had started high school. I had tasted something real, something transformative, and I couldn't go back to playing church.

Shared Experiences: When Faith Finds Adoptees

Kaitlin: Faith Despite the Wounds

I described Kristen's adoption story earlier. Her younger sister Kaitlin was also adopted by the same parents. They each had different birth mothers and fathers. Kaitlin was adopted through Bethany Christian Services and came home with her new parents when she was two days old. Her birth mother was of Columbian descent, and her birth father was a mix of predominately Puerto Rican.

In those two days before the agency placed her, they called her future adoptive mom to say that Kaitlin was having epileptic seizures caused by the birth mother's drug use. The agency asked if they still wanted to adopt her, and the answer from her mom was a resounding "YES!"

Growing up, she and Kristen got along well, and they even look like one another, though they aren't blood relatives. When she was young, Kaitlin's parents celebrated her adoption day every year with a cake. That is one of many good memories Kaitlin has from the past. She believes the reason for her great childhood is because of her loving and caring adoptive mom. She recognizes that her mom sacrificed a lot for her and Kristen, especially at Christmas when, although finances were tight, she always made sure they had presents.

In general, life was good for Kaitlin. She dealt with anger issues as a teenager through a couple of years of counseling.

As she grew up in Florida, her adoption agency would forward gifts and letters to her from her birth mom, keeping the birth mom's contact information confidential. In her senior year of high school, Kaitlin sent her birth mom a graduation photo. Somehow, based on that picture, her birth mom found Kaitlin on Facebook and asked if she could come to her graduation. Kaitlin agreed, and that would be the first time Kaitlin met Maria, who resided in New York.

Maria showed up with her current husband, even though Kaitlin had not agreed to that addition. Having them around made the night before her graduation tense, awkward, and basically a mess. Kaitlin said, "Maria's visit ruined my graduation."

She describes her birth mom as a sad, emotional person who used drugs during her pregnancy and afterwards. Because of the difficulties in their relationship, Kaitlin no longer has contact with her birth mom and has blocked her on social media. Even though she addressed her issues with anger as a teenager, Kaitlin readily admits she still has a lot of anger towards Maria that has never been resolved.

Kaitlin's birth father passed away in 2019 before she had a chance to meet him. She has learned that he had severe anger issues and was described as being not a very nice person. In addition, Kaitlin has located half siblings on both her mom and dad's sides of the family. As of now, all the siblings are nervous about meeting one another, so they just follow one another at a distance on social media. None of them want to communicate directly with her, and she feels the same way about them.

Today Kaitlin struggles with anxiety and depression that she manages with medication. Even though she struggled with some of her specific circumstances, Kaitlin believes adoption can be a blessing. Now that she knows the story of her birth parents, she recognizes that God protected her from her birth mother's drinking and drug use. Her many good memories of her mom also make her thankful that God placed her in the family that He did.

Despite all the challenges—or perhaps because of them—Kaitlin found faith. "I know God saved me," she says. "Not just spiritually, but literally. If I had stayed with my birth mom, I don't think I would have survived. My adoptive mom's faith showed me what real love looks like. It's choosing someone even when they're difficult. It's saying yes when everyone else says no. That's what God does for us, right? He chooses us even though He knows we're a mess."

Ingris: Letters to Heaven

Ingris was born in Honduras in 1977. At the age of five, she and her younger ten-month-old brother, Mickey, came from an orphanage to the United States. Their birth mother had passed away, and her father had placed her, Mickey, and an older sister in the orphanage.

Her adoptive parents already had two biological sons, Jeff and Chad, and they wanted to adopt a girl. An adoption agency had previously offered them two young girls, but the birth mother changed her mind. It was after that experience when they chose to adopt Ingris and Mickey.

Because she was adopted at the age of five, Ingris always knew she was adopted. Memories of being in the orphanage have stayed with her, especially regarding food, which Ingris remembers hiding, since there was never enough. As a child, Ingris missed her birth mother and wrote letters to her in heaven. "Writing those letters to heaven was my way of praying before I really knew how to pray," Ingris reflects. "I would tell my birth mother everything—about school, about feeling different, about missing her even though I couldn't really remember her. I think God heard those letters. I think He was teaching me that He's the Father who never leaves."

She also dreamed about being reconnected with her older birth sister, Johanna, who was also supposedly adopted. Even though Ingris has searched, it seems Johanna has disappeared, and the search for her has so far produced no results.

Even though Ingris always understood she had been adopted, her adoptive parents didn't openly discuss this fact with her. Her adoptive family is Christian, and she grew up attending a Methodist church. While growing up, Ingris's brother Chad was closest to her in age and always laughed at her jokes. This made her feel closest to him.

Ingris had a seventeen-year teaching career, and at the age of forty, she left her position teaching English Language Arts at a brick and mortar elementary school. Even though she wasn't ready to retire, Ingris had been feeling a tremendous amount of stress from teaching. Drinking heavily at night had become her routine, but that led to an inability to sleep. At that point, she chose to begin counseling with a Christian therapist. Currently Ingris is on medication for mild depression and severe panic disorder.

After leaving the in-person teaching position, Ingris eventually took a job teaching online seventh grade science. Now she is forty-seven, lives in Texas, and has been in this online teaching role for about five years. She is married to George, who also happens to be adopted. They have two sons; one is twenty-seven, and the other is twelve years old. Teaching online has been a blessing because she teaches from home and has been less stressed. The flexibility also allows her to attend events for her own children.

"My faith is complicated," Ingris admits. "I believe in God, but trusting Him is hard when your first experience of life is abandonment. My dad put us in an orphanage. I get that he couldn't care for us after Mom died, but understanding and feeling are two different things. Some days I trust God completely. Other days I'm still that five-year-old hiding food because I'm not sure there will be any tomorrow."

Ingris believes God has a plan for her life. She states she is a very empathetic person, does a lot of thinking, and speculates that her primary mission is to be a good mom for her two boys. She also says she feeds off the emotions of those around her.

When reflecting on lessons she's learned about life and coming to terms with her adoption, Ingris recounts being raised with the idea that if you fell, you got up, brushed yourself off, and got on with life. "But here's what I've learned," she continues. "Sometimes God supports us through our own strength. He gave me resilience. He gave me the ability to survive. And now, He's teaching me that I don't always have to be strong. That's hard for an adoptee to learn—that it's safe to be weak, safe to need help, safe to trust. My faith is growing as I learn to let God support me in ways no human ever has."

Mickey: Wrestling with God and Identity

Mickey is Ingris' younger brother and was also adopted from Honduras. Although he was given the name Miguel by his birth father, at age fifteen, he legally changed his name to Mickey. When reflecting about his thoughts on adoption while growing up, Mickey does not have a lot of memories but does remember hearing the word "adopted" as a young child and "Adoption Day" being celebrated with a party for the first couple of years. But like with Ingris, the circumstances of his adoption were not often discussed.

It was his external physical characteristics, which were different from those of his adopted family, that most often forced Mickey to acknowledge the fact of his adoption. One vivid memory stands out, which is when a neighbor in East Texas told him that although he was genetically Hispanic, he should still mark "white" on school forms.

Mickey is confident that he and his birth sister Ingris experienced early childhood trauma in Honduras. They've both had their struggles as adults, particularly with substance use. When they were growing up, Ingris often reminded him that they were adopted—perhaps as a way to protect and prepare him for whatever he might be feeling.

Among his siblings, Mickey feels most similar in personality and values to his oldest brother Jeff, who is eight years older. When they were growing up, Mickey would have described Jeff as his hero. "I always looked up to him." When Jeff invited him to tag along, it always made him feel welcomed and included. He reiterates, "We got along really well."

Over time, Mickey felt there was a growing distance between him and the rest of the family. In his thirties, he took a 23andMe DNA test to begin searching for his older sister Johanna or any other biological relatives. So far, he hasn't located any close family.

His faith journey has been full of both tension and growth. The tension came primarily from the words spoken at church about God's love for all people and the words he heard throughout the week putting down people who looked like he did. "I grew up in a white Methodist church in East Texas as one of the only brown kids," he says. "Every Sunday, I'd hear that God loves everyone. But Monday through Saturday, I'd hear negative comments about 'those Mexicans.' I learned early that church people could say one thing and live another."

It wasn't until his twenties, while serving in the military, that Mickey encountered real, embodied faith. "I met a chaplain who was different. He didn't just preach about God's truth; he lived it. He told me God wasn't trying to make me white or force me to fit in. He said God made me Honduran on purpose—that even my adoption was part of His plan. That was the first time I thought maybe God actually wanted me as I am."

"My faith isn't perfect," Mickey says. "I still struggle with trusting God completely—that fear of abandonment runs deep. But I've learned that God is more patient with my doubts than most people are. He keeps showing up. Keeps proving He's not going anywhere. That's what I needed: a God who won't give me away."

Though Mickey says he felt love and joy 90% of the time growing up, the remaining 10% was marked by inner conflict—especially around his Hispanic identity. During college, Mickey studied in New York City and found himself surrounded by a vibrant mix of cultures, and something shifted. "I realized life is largely about circumstance," he says. "And I'm really grateful I was adopted."

Now Mickey lives in Pennsylvania with his wife and two children, one stepson and one biological son. He owns a videography business and serves in the National Guard, where he uses his skills in Public Affairs. He often thinks about his birth father and the story he'd always been told about how he gave Ingris and

Mickey up so they could have a better life. As a father now, Mickey can't imagine making that choice.

He admits to carrying lingering fears of abandonment—an anxiety that he might one day be able to leave behind. But his perspective has grown: "As the world gets smaller, my heart gets larger."

Your Journey: Finding Your Spiritual Identity

No matter how loving and smooth an adoption is, it's difficult to escape the reality that adoption makes life a little complicated. Obviously I believe the complication is a thousand times worth the effort, but when we don't acknowledge the very real questions, doubts, and insecurities that adoption brings, there's a piece of our story that isn't quite settled. A big part of the complication adoption may bring is that of identity.

Language describing God as our Father and saying that He has adopted us as His children can add to the complicated feelings we have, not only about our specific situation, but also in embracing a life of faith and living in relationship with God. These are common truths that I believe to be universal for adoptees.

What Never Changes

- Your identity in Christ stays the same, even if your name changed
- You are grafted into God's family tree
- Your belonging is not in question
- Your adoption story has purpose

Maybe you call yourself an adopted child of God, or maybe you're not ready to take that step. Either way, consider these questions as you think about the topic of your identity.

Reflection Moment

1. Have you had a sense of God speaking to you? Some may call this a "call." Did you respond to His voice?
2. How has adoption affected your faith, either pushing you closer to God or creating more doubts about Him?
3. Where do you see God affirming the specific way that He created you with an intentional identity? How can you embrace this and grow deep in the way He has made you?
4. What matters most to you: being chosen, loved, safe, or permanent?

Significant Next Steps

- **Double Adoption Meditation:** Close your eyes. Picture being placed with your adoptive parents. See them look at your face and feel their joy. Now see God there too, knowing all about you and specifically blessing you, saying, "This is my beloved child." Feel being twice chosen.
- **Acknowledge Shared Traits:** Perhaps you feel that you are very different from your adoptive family. Maybe you look very different from them, or your hobbies and interests don't align with theirs. Embrace the beauty of this diversity. Even if the differences feel overwhelming, look for similarities and write them down. They may feel small, but as you continue

thinking, there may be more than you first would have identified.

- **Build a Diverse Network:** One of the most beautiful aspects of God's creation is that His creativity is evident all around. Seek out people from different backgrounds than your adoptive family, even who are different from what you know of your biological family. Being intentional to develop relationships with people who aren't in our everyday circles expands our understanding of ourselves and this amazing world God created.

Prayer

Dear God,

Thank You that You have always been pursuing me, always been calling me, always been claiming me as Your own. Heal the parts of me that struggle to trust Your permanence. When I fear You might change Your mind about my worth, remind me that Your adoption of me is sealed with the blood of Jesus. Remind me of the price You paid to make me Yours.

Thank You that my earthly adoption was not a mistake but part of your divine plan. Help me to live as one who is deeply known and deeply loved. Give me courage to share my story so others can find their way to You.

I entrust my entire self to You. Impress upon me that Your deep love will outlast any earthly love and any earthly doubt about who I am.

In the name of Jesus, who was also raised by an adoptive father,

Amen.

A Final Thought

That night at the Free Fare concert, when I tore off my ticket corner and won that album, I thought God was just answering a teenager's silly prayer. Now I understand that He was doing so much more. He was showing a young adoptee that she was seen, heard, and chosen—again, this time by a God who is not only real but deeply involved in my life.

Your spiritual adoption doesn't erase the complexity of your earthly adoption. Instead, it reframes it. God can use all of the questions you have about your birth story and bring healing and answers through your spiritual relationship with Him. All of the hard experiences you have endured, the rejection and the losses, are restored by His love.

This truth about God has changed my entire perspective on adoption and is a main reason I wanted to write this book. My prayer is that you will understand you are not just adopted, you are twice-chosen—once by parents who said yes when they could have said no, and eternally by a God who says you were worth the sacrifice of His Son.

God Is Your True Father

When "Father" Is a Complicated Word

WHAT HAPPENS to your heart when someone says the word "father"? Does it warm with memories of safety and love? Does it ache with absence? Does it become confused with competing images: birth father unknown, adoptive father trying, stepfathers coming and going? Or do your emotions simply feel blank, like encountering a word in a foreign language you never learned?

For adoptees, "father" is rarely simple. We might have a birth father we've never met, whose absence shapes us as much as his presence might have. We might have an adoptive father who loves us fiercely but sometimes feels like he's jumping into a role he doesn't feel prepared to play. We might have stepfathers, foster fathers, or no fathers at all.

On Sundays when the preacher tells us to pray to "Our Father who art in heaven," the worship leader sings about running into "Daddy's arms," and the Bible study teaches about God as "Abba Father"—literally Greek for "Daddy"—do you sit there, trying to connect with a metaphor that feels more like a minefield?

Even though I've had several types of "fathers," I've come to understand that this confusion and wide experience of who fathers are may be exactly why God chose to reveal Himself as Father. What if He knew that those of us with the most complicated father stories would be the ones who most need Him to fulfill the role of father? What if every disappointment delivered by an earthly father was meant to drive us into the arms of the only Father who never fails?

Each one of our adoption stories, with all of the variety of father-shaped holes and imperfect father figures, have uniquely prepared us to understand what it truly means to be a child of God. Let me tell you how I discovered that my search for earthly belonging was really a search for my heavenly Father, and how finding Him changed my perspective completely.

My Journey: From Father Wounds to Father Healing

The Question of Belonging

Let's take a moment and think about orphans who are given up by their birth parents and are never adopted into another family. My heart breaks for these children who spend their entire childhood in an orphanage, without being attached to a family and never feeling the love of any parents, siblings, grandparents, aunts, or uncles. I have often considered the difficult experience it must be to cope mentally, spiritually, and emotionally with being so alone.

Do these children and others who have families who are uninvolved in their lives ever come to realize the great news that we can be adopted by God? Does someone tell them? Do they figure it out on their own? Ephesians 1:4-6 states,

For he chose us in him before the creation of the world to be holy and blameless in his sight. In love he predestined us for adoption to sonship through Jesus Christ, in accordance with his pleasure and will—to the praise of his glorious grace, which he has freely given us in the One he loves.

As a child, I don't remember feeling alone, because I always had my mom. After she and my dad divorced when I was about four, it was just the two of us. Mom was the center of my universe. We had no family living near us, and my grandparents were a couple of hours away, so we didn't see them often. My life completely revolved around mom. She was my caretaker, provider, teacher, and even my companion. It wasn't that I didn't have friends, because I did, but I spent most of my time with mom.

Looking back, I realize I was one of those children searching for a father without even knowing it. My adoptive father George loved me, I know he did. But something happened in their marriage when I was so young that I don't even remember him being there. The divorce meant I lost not just a father, but the very concept of what a father should be.

I know from photos and early childhood memories that I was dedicated at First Baptist Church in Clearwater. My mom was a Christian and taught Sunday School up until her divorce. She told me through the years that she prayed for me daily.

God's Part

I shared earlier about becoming a Christian at the Free Fare concert and that church activities became a key part of my life while my faith deepened. Even though my faith grew even then, I didn't immediately begin making connections between the significant part that God played in my adoption and the role He plays in the lives of all those who are in need. We read in James 1:27, "Religion that God our Father accepts as pure and faultless is this: to look after orphans and widows in their distress and to keep oneself from being polluted by the world." God calls us to join Him in caring for widows and orphans. To me that means that God knows they are vulnerable and need extra love and care.

I'm not sure we always recognize the ways that God is with us, but we can trust that He is. There are moments and circumstances when He reveals the way He is caring, and those are revelations we can hold onto and use to strengthen our faith. For some, faith comes easy. This is especially true for children, who are pure and trusting. It is often when we grow into adults and encounter more people who have a lack of faith and belief in God that we become skeptical. It's common to question what we once believed and even allow others to influence our foundation of faith.

I haven't been immune to such questions about faith, but I have remained steady in confidence that God is real and near. Along the way, there have been spiritual turning points, and these stand out as important moments of clarity and focus. The period of time after I accepted Jesus as my Savior was an especially important time of growth. My faith deepened, and I experienced a thirst for God's Word. As I said in the previous chapter, the Living Bible, which was especially popular at that time, drew me closer to God, because the translation was easy to understand. I remember devouring everything written in it.

Something More

As I grew in my faith, I continued to seek something more. While I was participating in a Lutheran youth retreat, Pastor Paul spoke about the "something more" I desired. After the service, my friends and I cornered him to ask questions. He suggested we read some books that would point us in the right direction. The classic *Nine O'Clock in the Morning* by Dennis J. Bennett was one such book. I consumed each page, excited to read about the gifts of the Holy Spirit and the power and authority that God promised to those who believed in Him. It was life changing.

But there was something else I was seeking—something I couldn't quite name. I threw myself into church activities, youth group, choir, every place I could find to be involved. I was looking for something, someone. I didn't realize it then, but I was looking for the Father I'd never really had.

After marrying at the young age of eighteen, I fell away from the church, rarely attending. I distinctly recall a turning point where I felt God speaking to my heart and saying, "Either you are going to keep going in this same direction, away from me, or you can make the decision to do a 180 degree turn and return to serve me." I decided that even if my husband wouldn't attend church, I would.

The interesting thing about that moment was how God identified Himself to me. He didn't say "away from church" or "away from faith." He said "away from ME." His call was personal. It was relational. It was a Father calling His daughter home.

Through the years I've seen my share of both good times and difficult times. I leaned on my faith in God, knowing He loved me and had a plan for my life. But even when times were difficult, as life can be, I felt His presence. I was blessed with family and friends who loved and supported me, holding me up when I wasn't sure I could go on.

I'm sure you have faced your fair share of difficulties, like I have. Some of mine included relationship and marriage problems, which, as I've mentioned previously, led to my divorce and made me a single mom of two boys who needed much attention. As they grew, so did the behavior problems, both at home and school: drug use, stealing, mental health issues, anger, resentment, and the list went on and on. My days felt not only difficult, but also exhausting. Sometimes I felt like I was drowning in a lake, and I couldn't even see the shore on the other side.

During my divorce, I remember crying out to God one night, "Where are you? I need a Father! I need someone to protect me, to provide for me, to tell me it's going to be okay!" In that moment, I heard Him whisper to my heart, "I AM your Father. I have always been your Father. Let me be what you need."

I sought godly counsel and guidance from Christian mental health professionals through those hard times, and of course, God was faithful. Somehow God always let me know He was by my side. My circle of friends encouraged me and gave me support as I healed from the darkness of the previous years. Eventually I made it across that lake and finally entered a season of rest and renewal.

Noel

I'd been a single mother for about eight or nine years when my friend Cindy from church asked if she could give my phone number to the recently divorced brother of her friend Marilyn. His name was Noel. At that point I didn't have much hope of meeting a good Christian man. But I agreed, saying to go ahead and give him my number. A couple of weeks passed, and then he called. We had a long conversation with plenty of humor. He asked me out for dinner on Friday night. I was so excited but tried my best to act cool, which felt nearly impossible, since this kind of excitement was the kind that makes butterflies flutter in your stomach. I walked around for four days with a smile on my face, looking forward to the upcoming date.

I am tall and was convinced there was something in the water that was producing only short men in my area of central Florida. When I opened the door that Friday night, I was both surprised and mesmerized by how tall and handsome Noel was.

We drove to Anna Maria Island for dinner in his blue Nissan 280Z T-top sports car with bucket seats. Talk about making a good first impression with a jazzy car! It was such an enjoyable night that I hoped it would never end.

The next morning, Noel called to invite me to a Southern Gospel sing that evening at a local church. He would be participating in a quartet made up of his sister and a couple of friends. I quickly accepted the invitation, then called a Baptist friend to ask her what to wear to a gospel sing.

He picked me up again in his fancy car, and off we went. It was a wonderful evening and my first exposure to Southern Gospel music. I loved it. Some songs were fast and peppy; others were slow and thoughtful, with a meaningful message that touched your heart. Noel's baritone voice captivated me with its smooth, strong, and rich tone.

Our two churches were practically within walking distance of one another. He attended a Nazarene church, and I attended an Episcopal church. After service the following Sunday, several friends, including my best friend Fran, and I went to a nearby sandwich shop for lunch. I had invited Noel to join us. He showed up, and we had a wonderful time chatting and visiting. My church friends quizzed him, checking him out. After he left, Fran, who has a great sense of humor, declared that she didn't think he was a serial killer. Thank God for friends!

When I arrived home after lunch, I checked my answering machine and found a message from Noel. That seemed odd, since we had just left one another. I returned his call and found out that he had tickets to see country singer John Michael Montgomery in Tampa that night. Lucky for me, his date had just called and cancelled. He apologized profusely for asking me out at the last minute, but he thought we might have a good time together at the concert. I am not a stupid person, so of course I said yes! This would be our fourth date in just three days, which was a pretty good outcome for what had started out as one blind date.

After that weekend, we talked on the phone every day. We discovered we both worked in the same small town, with his office on the north side of Interstate 4 and my office on the south side. That made it easy to sometimes meet for lunch. He also came over regularly to my home for dinner. I enjoyed his company and conversations more and more each time we met. It felt like God had used that blind date to bring us together.

What struck me most about Noel was how different he was from other men I'd known. He proved to be steady, reliable, and consistent. When he said he would call, he called. When he made a plan, he followed through. He showed me something I'd never experienced: what a godly man actually looked like in daily life.

Once we became more serious, whenever his quartet traveled to sing at churches and events, I joined them. We met wonderful Christians by visiting many churches of various denominations. Since it would be a second marriage for both of us, we intentionally dated for two years before deciding to marry. My parents and friends all loved him, and they enjoyed being a part of our two-year courtship. Mom and Dad joked that the gas grill they gave us was part of my dowry.

From the very beginning, Noel has been the single greatest blessing in my life. He describes himself as an introvert, which compliments my extrovert personality. After years of uncertainty, I felt complete once we found each other. I was whole. Not only because of a faith that had matured, but because of the person God had placed in my path who would become my husband and lifelong partner. He was a godly man who complemented me and shared the same faith. And it was also a blessing to inherit Noel's three wonderful daughters.

God's Plans

All of this led me to realize something important. From the moment I was born, God had a plan for my life. The good news is that He has a plan for your life too. Maybe you didn't know that, or maybe you have heard that but haven't believed it is true.

Jeremiah 29:11 says, "'For I know the plans I have for you,' declares the Lord, 'plans to prosper you and not to harm you, plans to give you hope and a future.'" Now if you ask me, that's some very significant good news. Can you comprehend that the God of the universe loves and cares about you, and that He has plans for your life?

Looking back, I can see how God was fathering me all along:

- Through my grandfather James, who showed me masculine gentleness.
- Through Frank, my godfather, who provided stability.
- Through Pastor Paul, who pointed me to spiritual truth.
- Through church leaders, who guided my growth.
- Through counselors, who helped me heal.
- Through Noel, who showed me covenant love.

Each of these men was a glimpse of the Father heart of God. None of them were perfect, but each reflected some aspect of how God fathers His children. Let's look at more adoption stories for clues about how we too can sort through our adoptions, tackle our feelings and the tough issues, and receive the healing and wholeness God wants us to experience.

Shared Experiences: Finding Father Through the Journey

Chad: When Adoption Multiplies Love

Chad was six years old when his parents, Nancy and Dale, adopted two children from Honduras. We met his adopted siblings, Ingris and Mickey, in the previous chapter, and we will meet more of the family in this chapter. The challenge of the language barrier stands out to Chad as one of the first memories of having Ingris and Mickey join their family. Not being able to communicate with his new siblings was incredibly difficult. They spoke no English, and his family didn't speak Spanish. In the beginning, it was frustrating trying to communicate.

"Watching my dad with Ingris and Mickey taught me what real fatherhood looks like," Chad reflects. "He didn't treat them differently than Jeff and me. When Mickey struggled with his identity, Dad was there. When Ingris had attachment issues with Mom, Dad was the bridge. He showed me that being a father isn't about biology—it's about showing up."

As a six-year-old, Chad didn't realize the part God played in the adoption of his two siblings. Now he understands the miracle it was that God moved the two small children out of Honduras to a safe and loving family. Because Chad is just one year older than his sister, they bonded and shared the same friends in high school. He is incredibly grateful for both Ingris and Mickey, who have been blessings in their family. Even today, he enjoys the time he spends with both of their families. Every other year, their entire family meets up at Christmas at a different location, such as Branson, Missouri or Fort Worth, Texas.

As of our interview, Chad is forty-eight years old and a principal of an elementary school of four hundred students, from pre-school through fifth grade. Even though he has a staff of sixty-five, he and the Physical Education teacher are the only male staff in the school. This disproportionate influence in the building makes Chad feel like he needs to intentionally be a positive male role model for the young children. It's his belief that God has called him to be a principal in a public school, and he takes this calling seriously.

"I see kids all the time who don't have fathers," Chad explains. "Or they have multiple father figures coming in and out of their lives. I try to be consistent for them, to show them what stability looks like. My dad taught me that. He taught me that sometimes the most important thing a man can do is simply be there, day after day, no drama, just presence."

Chad's work has taught him a lot about patience, especially in this post-Covid world, where there is a mental health crisis amongst school-age children. As an educator, he sees the connection between ADHD and children who are not closely parented. In addition, children spend an enormous amount of time on screens, which, in his opinion, prevents them from knowing how to be bored. From his experience, boredom equals imagination, which is needed to explore and live creatively.

"God as Father makes sense to me because I watched my earthly father love kids who didn't share his DNA as much as the ones who did. That's what God does: He adopts us all, loves us all, provides for us all. My dad showed me God's heart."

As he summarized his thoughts about having adopted siblings, Chad says one of the most important lessons he has learned is to listen to God and be grateful to spend time together. Adoption isn't always easy, and it's crucial to love unconditionally, showing the same love towards all children, whether biological or adopted. Doing this requires patience, boundaries, and consistency.

Nancy & Dale: Learning to Parent Adopted Hearts

Next, let's hear the experience of Ingris and Mickey's adoption from their adoptive parents, Nancy and Dale. I found it fascinating to get the perspective of everyone in the family. Talking to each family member provided a complete description of adoption from several angles.

Nancy and Dale already had two boys but had always wanted a girl, so they applied to adopt through the Casa de Esperanza de los Niños agency in Houston, Texas. Soon after, they were offered two girls, whom they accepted and quickly made plans to travel to Honduras to meet. The night before they were to fly to Honduras, they were staying at an airport hotel when they received a call from the agency advising them that the birth mother had changed her mind. They hadn't been told this was a possibility and were devastated. Clothes had been purchased for the girls and rooms decorated, and now they weren't needed.

They returned home to regroup and wait for the next opportunity. Within about four months they were contacted again by the agency, offering them a five-year-old girl named Ingris and her brother, an ten-month-old boy named Miguel. The agency needed an answer that same day. They prayed all day and decided to move forward with their adoption. Within a month, Nancy and Dale were on their way to Honduras.

Once in the country, they met with the lawyer, along with the birth father, who told them his wife had died from stomach cancer. He felt like he had to give up his children. Only once they arrived did they learn that this man also had a third child, an older daughter Johanna. She had been up for adoption as well, but they later learned the father changed his mind and took her home.

Nancy shared that on the day she and Dale first saw their two adopted children, she was immediately overwhelmed with love for both of them. She had thought it would take time to grow to love them, but that wasn't the case.

"I understood in that moment what God feels when He adopts us," Nancy says. "It's not a gradual growing of love. It's instant, overwhelming, complete. Those were my children from the moment I saw them, just like we're God's children from the moment He calls us."

When they met him, Miguel was severely malnourished and near death. Nancy and Dale quickly fed him the food they had brought and shared supplies for his care. While there, both children came down with chicken pox, and Miguel also had a secondary infection. Nancy ended up staying in Honduras for three weeks, but after one week in Honduras, Dale had to return to the States.

"Leaving Nancy there with two sick children was one of the hardest things I've ever done," Dale recalls. "But I knew God had called us to these children. I had to trust Him to be their Father when I couldn't be there. I prayed every night, 'God, be the Father to them that their birth father couldn't be. Be the Father to them through Nancy until I can get back to them.'"

When the time came to leave Honduras, Nancy had to go to the American Consulate and take the children with her. She took a friend along to help with Ingris and to hold Miguel, because he was still sick. Fearing their poor health would prevent them from being able to travel out of the country, Nancy had them wait across the room while she was interviewed. Miraculously, the official approved their paperwork without seeing Miguel up close.

That wasn't the end of needing to appear healthy. At the Houston airport, customs officials questioned if Miguel's case of chicken pox was actually smallpox. Ultimately the agents allowed Nancy and the children to enter the country but stipulated that Miguel needed to see the doctor the next day and to expect a follow-up call from the CDC. The call never came. At the airport, when Dale finally saw the children, he thought Miguel was a different child, because he had gained so much weight and looked healthy.

"The transformation was miraculous," Dale says. "In three weeks, he went from being near death to being healthy. That's what the Father's love does. It transforms. It heals. It brings life where there was death."

In my earlier telling of Miguel's story, I explained that Miguel changed his name to Mickey. He initiated this discussion when he was a senior in high school, and Dale and Nancy were not opposed. They went to court and changed his name to Mickey, which was what he'd been unofficially called since he arrived into the family.

Ingris had some counseling as a child, but Nancy and Dale do not remember any specific diagnosis being shared with them. "Dale has been amazing with attachment issues," Nancy reflects. "Ingris struggled to attach to me—there were control battles, trust issues, the typical stuff adoptive moms face with older adopted children. But Dale never gave up. He was the steady presence that showed both kids what a father's love looks like. Patient, consistent, unchanging."

Regarding any search their adopted children might want to conduct, Nancy said she wouldn't have a problem with them looking for biological family members. In addition, Mickey has talked about making a documentary about a child from Honduras being adopted, which would mirror his own story.

Nancy said she wouldn't change anything about the adoption process but would have sought more help with how to handle the behavior problems they encountered. They do not feel they were adequately prepared specifically for international adoption. When they encountered discrimination against their adopted children and insensitive comments, they did not know the best way to handle that challenge.

"People would ask the most inappropriate questions right in

front of the kids," Nancy remembers. "'Are those your real children?' 'How much did they cost?' 'Do they know their real parents?' I wanted to scream, 'We ARE their real parents!' Dale and I are the ones who showed up every day. We're the ones who held them through nightmares, who fought for their education, who loved them through their struggles. That's what real parents do."

If they had been more educated about conversations to have and things to do, they wonder if those situations could have been handled differently.

"Being an adoptive father taught me about God's Father heart in ways being a biological father didn't," Dale adds. "With Jeff and Chad, there was never a question of belonging—they looked like us, acted like us. But with Ingris and Mickey, we had to be intentional about creating belonging. We had to choose them every single day. And that's what God does with us. He chooses us every single day, especially on the days when we don't look like we belong in His family."

Jeff: The Oldest Brother's Perspective

Jeff was nine years old when his parents decided to adopt a girl to join him and his younger brother Chad. He remembers numerous trips to their adoption agency in Houston and then the plans for his mom and dad to go to Honduras that first time. That was when they expected to adopt two girls, ages two years and ten months. The agency had provided photos of the girls, and they had bought clothes for them, preparing for their arrival. They were all excited about the girls becoming part of their family. As Nancy and Dale described in their account, at the last minute, the birth mother changed her mind. Even though they had never met the girls, Jeff said that experience felt like a death.

Sometime later his parents were offered Ingris and her

brother Miguel. Once his parents arrived back home to Texas, the newness and shine of new siblings quickly wore off. Jeff remembers their first Christmas together and feeling like the two new siblings got a ton of presents, way more than he and Chad did.

"I was jealous at first," Jeff admits. "I mean, I was nine. I'd been the oldest, the special one. Now there were these new kids getting all the attention."

After a year had passed, the family had adjusted, and it no longer seemed like the siblings were adopted. It felt like Ingris and Mickey had always been part of their family. Jeff says that his adopted siblings have been a huge blessing, and he can't imagine their family without them.

"Watching my parents navigate adoption gave me a whole different view of God," Jeff reflects. "I saw them love kids who tried to push them away. I saw them provide for kids who didn't trust them. I saw them stay faithful when it was hard. That's what God does for us. He fathers us even when we're difficult to father.

"My parents showed me that family isn't about blood. It's about choice. God chose us before the foundation of the world, and my parents chose Ingris and Mickey. Every day, they chose them again. That's what good fathers and mothers do: they choose their children, again and again, no matter what."

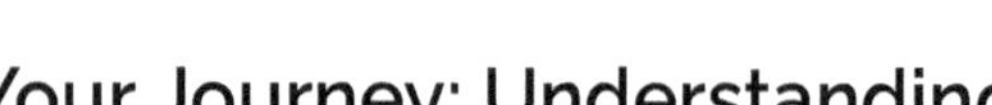

Your Journey: Understanding God as Father When Earthly Fathers Fail

The Father Wounds We Carry

Every adoptee I've met carries some kind of father wound. Maybe your birth father is a blank line on a certificate. Maybe your adoptive dad tried his best but never fully embraced that you were really his. Maybe you worked yourself to exhaustion trying to please a stepfather that never accepted you. We all have our version of being wounded.

These wounds are hurtful and impact our sense of safety and protection, and they also shape how we see God. I've heard so many adoptees say things like:

- "If my own father gave me away, wouldn't God do the same?"
- "I have to be perfect or He'll change His mind about me"
- "I can't get too close—it'll hurt too much when He leaves"

Here's what I learned after decades of working through this: God chose adoption language on purpose. He knew some of us would struggle with "Father." He knew we'd have wounds. And He still said, "This is how I want you to know Me." Why? Because He's the Father we needed all along. The One who redeems every failed father story. The One who fills every father gap.

Your earthly father story might be terrible. But it's not your only father story. You have a heavenly Father who's been pursuing you since before you were born, who chose you knowing exactly how much healing you'd need, who calls you His own and means it forever.

That's the Father you can trust. Even when trusting feels impossible.

Reflection Moment

1. Psalm 68:5 describes God as a "father to the fatherless." How can you draw comfort from this verse?

2. God not only knows about these wounds the word "father" carries; He also speaks directly to them. Take some time to read through the common shared emotions below and pray through the verses listed.

When we feel abandoned: *"Though my father and mother forsake me, the Lord will receive me"* (Psalm 27:10).

When we feel unnamed: *"I will give them an everlasting name"* (Isaiah 56:5).

When we feel rejected: *"See what great love the Father has lavished on us, that we should be called children of God"* (1 John 3:1).

God is not like earthly fathers. He never leaves. He always provides. His love isn't based on our performance. He actually knows us—not just *about* us, but deeply knows us.

3. What does it mean to you that the love the Father has for you will last forever?

4. List the attributes of earthly fathers. Now make a list of God as a Father. Notice where there are similarities and differences.

Significant Next Steps

- **Practice receiving.** This is hard for adoptees. Start small. Accept a compliment without deflecting. Let someone help without earning it.

- **Face the hurt you're carrying with honesty.**
  Name exactly how father-absence hurt you. It's time
  to stop pretending that everything is fine when it may
  not be. Set aside time to let the emotions flow
  through your mind. Recognize them, sit with the
  feeling they've brought, and then let them pass
  through.
- **Healing Prayer.** Although it may sound childish, the
  lap prayer can be a source of healing. Sit quietly and
  imagine yourself as a little kid climbing into God's
  lap. Don't talk. Just let yourself be held. Stay as long
  as you feel comfortable. Try it again and you may find
  it easier to stay longer.
- **Find a spiritual father,** an older Christian man who
  can show you what godly masculinity looks like. Not
  to replace anyone, just to model something healthy.

Prayer

Perfect Father,

I come to You with all my father wounds—the absence, the trying-but-failing, the almost-but-not-quite-right experiences. I bring You my confusion about what "father" even means, my fear that if I trust in You, I will only be disappointed again.

Thank You that You are not like earthly fathers. You never leave. You never give up. You never have a bad day. You never love me less. You chose me before I was born, pursued me when I ran, and paid the ultimate price to make me Yours.

Please heal the places inside of me that have been wounded. Where I expect abandonment, teach me Your faithfulness. Where I expect distance, draw me close. Where I expect disappointment, surprise me with Your goodness.

Thank You for every person You've used to father me—for grandfathers and godfathers, for mentors and ministers, for adop-

tive fathers who tried and stepfathers who stayed. Each one was a glimpse of You.

I am Your child. You are my Father. That is enough.

Amen.

A Final Thought

Every adoptee's journey to understanding God as Father is unique. Some see God's heart reflected clearly in an earthly father. Others must dig through layers of disappointment to find the Father who was always there.

But here's the beautiful truth: God chose to reveal Himself as Father knowing that many of His children would struggle with that very word. He knew there would be absent birth fathers and trying-hard adoptive fathers and complicated stepfathers.

And still, He says, "I will be your Father."

Not "I will be like a father" or "I will act fatherly." But "I will BE your Father."

In God's economy, adoption is not Plan B. It's not second best. This was His intentional choice from the beginning.

Moving Toward Wholeness

What Does "Whole" Look Like for an Adoptee?

TAKE a moment and imagine yourself completely whole. What would that look like? Would it mean no more questions about your birth story? No more triggers when someone asks about your "real" parents? No more anxiety when you hear about another adoptee finding devastating information about their birth family?

Or does wholeness look different than we think?

For years, I believed wholeness meant having all the answers. If I could just find my birth family, learn my medical history, understand why I was given up—then I'd be whole. Somewhere something changed, and I've come to a different understanding about feeling complete. It's not about erasing my adoption story or answering every question. Rather, my goal now is to integrate all the pieces of my story: the beautiful and the broken, the answered questions and those left unanswered. There's a joyful discovery in realizing that I am complete, even with missing pieces and unanswered questions.

Let me share a difficult truth: While being adopted does not automatically mean we will struggle with brokenness or mental health issues, statistics show we're more likely to. Not because there's something wrong with us, but because we've experienced a primal loss that many people never face. We've had to reconcile being part of our adoptive families, who have wanted us, and the biological families who gave us away. The ways our adoptive families make us feel special and yet the ways we may be different from them.

Let's talk honestly about the journey toward wholeness, including the mental health struggles many adoptees face, the generational patterns we might carry, and the healing that's possible when we stop pretending we're fine and start the real journey to being whole.

My Journey: Learning That Wholeness Includes Brokenness

The Statistics and the Stories

There are a variety of mental health issues that are common to adoptees, including depression, attachment wounds, grief, abandonment, trauma, anxiety, and behavioral issues. Adoptees also are at an increased risk of suicide compared to others.[*]

When I first read those statistics, I felt two things simultaneously: relief and fear. Relief because it meant I wasn't crazy or weak for struggling. Fear because it suggested maybe I am doomed to struggle forever. But what I've learned is that statistics tell us what's common, not what's inevitable. They show us we're not alone, not that we're hopeless.

---

[*] Theodora Blanchfield, "What Are the Mental Health Effects of Being Adopted?" Verywell Mind, 20 November 2025, https://www.verywellmind.com/what-are-the-mental-health-effects-of-being-adopted-5217799.

I am not a therapist; however, I have sought counseling off and on over the last thirty-plus years and have learned a thing or two from some great Christian counselors. In this chapter I will share my own personal stories and those of my siblings in order to shine a light on what some of the common issues may be.

Ardith

Ardith, my older half-sister, was diagnosed at a young age as bipolar. When our mother Maggie and Ardith's father Bob divorced for the second time, they both remarried quickly. Bob took Ardith, along with three of our siblings, to Texas with his new bride, where they remained for a month or so. Then, Bob left all four children at an orphanage, where they remained for a year. After a year, the orphanage told Bob he must take the children back or sign paperwork to allow them to be adopted. He picked up the children and drove straight to Pensacola, Florida, dropping them on Maggie's doorstep with the comment, "Now it's your turn!"

As an adult, Ardith made numerous attempts to take her own life. Even though Ardith was not adopted, she has always attributed her mental health issues to both the emotional and physical abuse from Maggie. The abandonment Ardith and her siblings experienced by being dumped at the orphanage might be comparable to the abandonment our sister Lynne and I experienced as adoptees.

Medications prescribed by her psychiatrist and medical doctor helped Ardith remain stable for most of the time I knew her. Ardith lived independently, even though she also relied on our older brother and sister-in-law for care and support. She was involved in her Methodist church, did volunteer work, wrote poetry, raised money each year for NAMI (National Alliance on Mental Illness), and had a circle of friends she socialized with and loved. Ardith was very outspoken about mental illness issues and the difficulties she had faced her entire life.

Ardith's refusal to let mental illness define her entire identity amazed me. Yes, she was bipolar. Yes, she had struggles. But she was also a poet, a volunteer, a friend, a church member, an advocate. She was broken AND whole, struggling AND contributing, sick AND living fully. She taught me that wholeness doesn't mean the absence of mental illness; it means living fully despite it.

In 2022, Ardith's behavior and depression led to several hospitalizations as her doctor tried desperately to make needed changes to her medications. Shockingly, at one point she was discharged from the hospital and just hours later attempted suicide by drinking toilet bowl cleaner. She made several more attempts over a short period of time, and in June of 2022, Ardith tragically succeeded. Her death was a sad ending to a life clouded with depression and serious mental health issues, and yet for the most part she lived her life well.

I grieved not just for Ardith, but for all of us who carry these heavy genetics, these inherited struggles. Her death forced me to face my own mental health more honestly. If my sister could live successfully with mental illness for decades and then suddenly succumb to it, what did that mean for me? For my children? For other adoptees who share these risks?

Lynne

Lynne, another one of my older half-sisters, also took her own life. Like myself, Lynne was given up for adoption at birth by our birth mother. As I mentioned earlier, Maggie, our birth mother, fought her own mental health struggles, and those genetics seem to have passed on to her children.

I have very little information about Lynne. What I do know I learned from her sister-in-law. Like my sister Ardith, Lynne was bipolar and battled depression. Her adopted mother was a nurse, and her father was a letter carrier. Five years after adopting Lynne, her parents adopted a son. That is about all I know of her young life. As an adult, Lynne had several failed marriages and moved away from Florida to live and work in North Carolina. She committed suicide by overdosing on pills.

Two women, my biological half sisters, ended their lives by their own choice. This pattern is impossible to ignore. Depression ran through our bloodline like a dark river, claiming victims. But patterns aren't prophecies. Rivers can be dammed, redirected, and crossed. That's what I decided to do—not to pretend the river didn't exist, but to build bridges over it.

Attachment

The subject of attachment is necessary to address when discussing adoption. If a baby is adopted at birth, chances are good that they will properly attach to the adoptive parents. If the child is placed later in life, even at three or four years of age, the attachment may be more difficult.

My deaf son Tommy was one and a half years old when the state removed him from his biological parents and placed him in a foster home. When he was three years old, his birth father agreed to give up custody so Tommy could be adopted. I remember our first meeting with him and the hours we shared together at a local zoo. He wasn't hesitant to go places with strangers and did not put up a fuss when we took him home later that week to spend the weekend with us.

The fifteen years he spent in my home were filled with some very difficult times. I believe his abused background made a huge impact on his life. From a young age, Tommy made some bad choices. Underlying his actions were severe anger issues and a propensity to lie. Counseling didn't seem to get his attention, and it sure didn't improve his behavior.

Looking back, I can see how Tommy's lack of appropriate stranger anxiety was actually a red flag. Children who have been through multiple caregivers often lose the ability to discriminate between safe and unsafe people. They'll go with anyone, because they've learned that caregivers are interchangeable. It's not a positive characteristic of resilience but of emotional resignation.

There are many factors that impact whether or not a child attaches to their adoptive parents. Unfortunately, there is no way to predict whether the child will adjust in a healthy way or not. I know my husband and I were in uncharted waters, taking it one day at a time and relying on the social workers and teachers for guidance.

You've probably heard some version of the line claiming that love conquers all. This is a romantic notion, and I like to believe it's true. In many ways I have seen how God's love is able to "cover a multitude of sins" (1 Peter 4:8), and I do believe God's love is so great that He overlooks our shortcomings to love us as we are.

At the same time, I came to understand with Tommy that my love alone wasn't enough to heal his attachment wounds. Adoptive parents often adopt believing they can love a child through any hardship. While this may be true, and while our love is unconditional, we still need tools, understanding, professional help, and most of all, realistic expectations. Wholeness for a child with severe attachment issues might look different than wholeness for a child adopted at birth. That doesn't mean it's less possible, but it does mean we need to be attentive to knowing when outside help is necessary.

Step By Step to Wholeness

At one point during my divorce, I struggled with depression, and for about a year, I took a prescribed antidepressant. Talk therapy, medication, exercise, and inner healing prayers brought me out of that cloud of depression. I remember describing to my therapist that the depression felt like a heavy cape that I could barely carry. It was a dark time in my life as I worked full-time while caring for my two sons. I leaned on my family, faith, and close friends as I worked through my struggles.

The antidepressant didn't make me happy. That's not what they do. It did lift the weight enough so that I could do the work of healing. It felt like I had someone holding up the heavy cape so I could stand up straight and start walking forward. Some people need that help for a season. Some need it for life. There's no shame in either.

At some point, after having worked through the depression to a degree, I made the decision to delve into the subject of my adoption. I was curious about many things, most of all why I had been given up by my birth mother. As a child I learned the subject of my adoption was taboo and not to be discussed. I kept my counseling sessions confidential from my parents, because I didn't want to do anything that would hurt or upset my mom. Sorting through my adoption would be something I needed to do quietly on my own.

I met with Betty, a petite, blonde licensed mental health professional who was a pastor's wife. Her Christian faith combined with her training were just what I needed. Together we sorted through what little information I had, and I started my journey of self-awareness. I looked forward to my counseling sessions, because they were a safe space to sort through a variety of issues.

"Tell me about being adopted," Betty said in one of our early sessions.

"Oh, it's fine," I replied automatically. "I had wonderful parents. I've been very blessed."

She waited. Therapists are good at waiting.

"I mean, I know I'm lucky. Some adoptees have terrible stories. Mine is good."

More waiting.

"I just wonder sometimes why she gave me away. But it's fine. It all worked out."

Betty leaned forward slightly. "What would happen if it wasn't fine?"

That question cracked something open in me. What would happen? Would I be ungrateful? Would I hurt my adoptive parents? Would I be a bad person? I started getting emotional, and my eyes filled with tears. For the first time in my life, I admitted that being adopted sometimes hurt. Even with wonderful adoptive parents. Even with a good life. The primal wound of being given away hurt.

"Adoption is a trauma that is often overlooked. It's not natural for a baby anything to be separated immediately from its mother," says Lesli Johnson, LMFT, a therapist who works with adoptees. "It's not OK to bring puppies home until they're eight weeks old, but with infants, we have this expectation that they're just supposed to fit in and belong."*

Inner Healing Prayers

I have discovered that some experiences I had as a child, a teen, or even as an adult have influenced my relationships. Before meeting Betty, I had previously worked with Jim and Barbara, a husband-and-wife team from my church. They were trained and experienced in the ministry of inner healing prayers and advised me to take some time at home to pray and make a list of hurts or difficult memories I had experienced since childhood. I easily filled several pages of things that came to mind. When I returned to discuss my list with them, we prayed over them, asking God to go back and heal those specific hurts.

During a time of inner healing prayer, Betty asked me to

---

* Blanchfield, "What Are the Mental Health Effects of Being Adopted?"

recognize that Jesus was present in the delivery room during my birth. "Where is He?" she asked.

I closed my eyes and could see the scene. "He's in the corner of the hospital room. He's smiling at me as I'm being born."

"What does He want to say to you?"

Through tears, I whispered what I heard in my spirit: "You're Mine. You've always been Mine."

Francis MacNutt wrote in his book *Healing* that "Inner healing is indicated whenever we become aware that we are held down in any way by the hurts of the past." *

Working with a therapist or inner healing counselor requires time and commitment. Healing sometimes happens instantly, but in other, more complicated scenarios, it may take time. I decided to slowly work through the insights revealed to me by the Holy Spirit.

Tommy

I shared earlier about my deaf son Tommy and the challenges we faced surrounding his struggles with attachment. There's more to Tommy's story, and I wish that we'd been told then what we came to know. My husband and I had been told by the social worker that Tom had been neglected and abused by his parents. There was little information available about the details of his living situation, other than he and his parents traveled up and down the eastern seaboard living like gypsies. He then spent one and a half years in a foster home before he came to live with us when he was three years old.

Naively we joined countless other adoptive parents who thought that love would be able to overcome any issues he might have. His father and I did everything we could to give him a

---

* Francis MacNutt, *Healing*. Ave Maria Press, 1 January 1974.

loving, stable family and a good education. But over the years, behavior problems became an ongoing routine.

The first time Tommy had a complete meltdown—screaming, throwing things, completely out of control—I called the social worker in tears. "What are we doing wrong?" I asked.

"You're not doing anything wrong," she said gently. "Tommy's brain was wired by trauma before you ever met him. You're trying to rewire it with love. That takes time, and sometimes it takes more than love."

That was our first lesson in trauma-informed parenting. We came to understand that Tommy's brain had developed in an environment of chaos and neglect. His neural pathways were shaped by survival, not security. That meant we weren't just parenting behaviors; we were trying to heal a nervous system that had learned the world was dangerous before he could even talk.

Tommy's behavioral problems surfaced early, as young as three, when he threw a chair at his preschool teacher. Over the years, we faced numerous conduct issues that were both difficult to handle and impossible to explain. Even at the Florida School for the Deaf and Blind, he stole a bicycle from the blind department and ended up in juvenile court. He was expelled multiple times during his two years there.

As a teenager, the incidents escalated. During an outing with our youth pastor, he stole a cassette tape from a Christian bookstore—which made no sense, since he couldn't hear. When family friends visited from out of town, he stole their van for a joyride to a friend's house. I began sleeping with my car keys tucked in my pillowcase, terrified he would take my car in the middle of the night.

There was more shoplifting—cigarettes from a grocery store that resulted in police being called—followed by his stubborn refusal to surrender his own car keys. He would lie and steal without any apparent conscience about his behavior.

The summer before his senior year, Tommy stole his father's car and wrecked it, which led to a six-week stay in a psychiatric hospital, followed by ongoing counseling after being discharged. As his parents, we did everything we could to help him succeed throughout the fifteen years he lived with us, and then, after the divorce, with me. His middle and high school years were an extremely difficult and stressful time for all of us.

I'm sharing my personal story in the hope that you might benefit and learn from what I have experienced. My story is unique because not only were his father and I both adopted at birth, but we also chose to adopt a child. Even though our experiences with Tommy were difficult, they did not change the fact that his father and I loved him very much. We cared for him the best we could, advocating for his education and seeking out much needed counseling.

We took him to church every Sunday and taught him our Christian beliefs. Once he turned eighteen and was an adult, he made choices that prevented him from living in my household. He knew my rules, and he chose not to obey them, knowing the consequences. I relied on the guidance of his psychologist, who confirmed the importance of being consistent. We needed firm boundaries, which is why we had a written contract spelling out the rules we had agreed on together. Tom's psychologist, his dad and I, and Tom all discussed the rules, and we all signed the contract.

When he broke the contract, he moved out and lived on his own. It was heartbreaking that after fifteen years, he was no longer part of my life. Over the years, we were estranged; at times he would surface, and I would then learn where he was living. But normally I wouldn't hear from him for long periods of time while he moved around frequently. I could not change the situation, and I had to learn to accept the way things were. Tommy was a long-time smoker, which eventually led to his death in August of 2022, when he sadly passed away from lung cancer at the young age of just forty-four years old.

Tommy's death brought a complicated grief. I grieved the son I had, the son I'd hoped he'd become, and the relationship we never got to repair. But his life taught me something crucial about wholeness: Sometimes wholeness means accepting what we cannot fix. Sometimes it means loving someone and letting them go. Sometimes it means recognizing that their brokenness is not our failure.

Navigating Life

I believe I am a stronger person after navigating through all that life has presented. I could have thrown in the towel and run away, but I didn't. Instead, I decided to plow through these chapters of my life as each unfolded. I leaned on my faith to deal with each situation. That hasn't been easy, and I don't claim to have always been successful, but somehow I've made it through.

All these life experiences have shaped me into the person I am today. There are parts of my life that I am happy with and others that I'm not. Like everyone, I have regrets and wish I had handled some things differently.

But this is what contributes to what I've come to understand about wholeness. Being whole is not about never making a mistake, living an easy life, and having no regrets. It's about integrating even those mistakes and regrets into our story. It may sound crazy, but being whole is not about being unbroken. Rather, wholeness is found by letting God use our broken places and living in peace even when we don't have all the answers.

One answer I am convinced of is that God knew what He was doing when arranging for me to be adopted. Understanding all that I know now, I'm glad I was adopted! I was chosen, not just by God, but by my adopted parents.

This is why I share my struggles. My goal is that sharing what I've learned will be an encouragement to you to dig deep and find the strength we all need to survive whatever life gives us.

Shared Experiences: Different Approaches to Healing

Greg: A Search That Brought Healing and Calling

Greg was born in Chicago, Illinois on December 9, 1959. His adoptive parents lived in Missouri but intentionally chose an adoption agency in Chicago. After spending his first five weeks in an orphanage, Greg was brought home to Missouri and adopted. Two years later, his parents adopted a baby girl. The unusual twist in their family story came when his adoptive mother, who had previously been unable to conceive, went on to give birth to two biological children after adopting both Greg and his sister.

Greg grows emotional when he recalls that his parents never hid the truth. Adoption was acknowledged, talked about, and honored in their home. That foundation of openness paved the way for the journey that came later.

At thirty-two, Greg took a long road trip from Missouri to Mississippi with a pastor friend. During hours of conversation, he found himself talking about his adoption in a way he never had before. By the time they returned home, he knew he was ready to search for his birth family.

That prompted him to join an adoption support group called Heart to Heart, where adoptees encouraged one another through the often painful and emotional process of searching. One evening, while watching a video about adoptees who navigate relationships with both birth mothers and adoptive mothers, Greg felt something shift inside. He knew it was time to take the next step.

With little progress from volunteer help, Greg set a personal goal. He would find his birth mother by his thirty-fifth birthday, just a couple of years from then. When the months passed without a breakthrough, he hired a licensed investigator. Several months later, the call came. The investigator had located his birth mother. Her name was Nancy.

Through the investigator, Greg sent a letter, praying she would want to meet. To his amazement, she had already begun searching for him.

As Nancy began to share her past, Greg learned she had carried a secret that shaped her life. One of four children, she became pregnant as a young woman. Her parents were furious and sent her to an unwed mothers' home in St. Louis. Her siblings never knew she had even been pregnant. They and her friends were told she had taken a job out of state.

After placing Greg for adoption, Nancy married, but she never told her husband about her first pregnancy. She later had two more children, a son and daughter. For decades she lived with the weight of a story she had never been able to speak aloud.

Nancy also revealed that Greg had actually been born on December 8, not December 9. It was common practice during that era to alter birth dates to help conceal an adoptee's identity.

Greg also learned that his birth father had passed away only six months after he was born.

One of the most remarkable parts of Greg's story is what happened years later. At the age of forty, Nancy felt called by God to become a pastor in the Presbyterian church. Her husband strongly opposed her decision and eventually divorced her. She enrolled at Perkins School of Theology at Southern Methodist University in Dallas.

At the same time, Greg answered his own call to ministry. Without knowing it, he attended that same school at the same time as his birth mother.

After comparing memories, they discovered they had both attended the school's Tuesday night dinners that cost one dollar. They had likely been in the same room many times, sitting just tables apart, unaware that mother and son were within arm's reach.

These details became sacred to them, proof that their paths had quietly crossed long before they finally met.

Nancy passed away in 2018, but Greg remains grateful they found one another when they did. The years they spent together were marked by truth, healing, and the mending of something that had been torn years earlier.

Greg also acknowledges how adoption shaped him emotionally. Over the years he has participated in inner healing prayer for adoption-related wounds that emerged later in life. Now, at sixty-six, he recognizes the patterns that grew out of his early story, including a tendency toward work addiction. He intentionally avoided alcohol for fear it might become a problem. Today he is married with two children, has served faithfully as a pastor, and is an accomplished author.

Greg is grateful for his adoption, his family, and the journey that ultimately led to his calling. Yet he describes adoption with an image that resonates with many adoptees.

"Adoption is like coming into a movie halfway through. Everyone else has seen the beginning. You arrive in the middle and spend much of life trying to understand what happened before you stepped into the story."

Greg's life is proof that the missing pieces can be found, truth can be redeemed, and God can weave healing into the deepest questions of our beginnings.

Multiple Siblings' Story: When Genetics and Environment Collide

As I've pieced together my birth family's story, I've learned about my four siblings who were raised by our birth mother, Maggie.

My oldest brother, Robert, joined the Air Force at eighteen, likely to escape the chaos at home. My sister Ardith, whose struggle with mental health I've shared earlier, was removed from the home at sixteen after reporting abuse. My brother Tommy lied about his age to join the Navy early. My sister Amber was kicked out on her eighteenth birthday.

Each developed their own coping mechanisms:

- Robert became hyper-independent, cutting off most family contact.
- Ardith struggled with bipolar disorder but built a support network.
- Tommy struggled to settle down in any one place.
- Amber found stability through her faith and creating her own family.

Lynne was my fifth sibling and was the one also given up to an adoptive family.

What strikes me is that we six siblings—two adopted out, four raised by Maggie—all carry wounds. But the type of wound differs. Those of us who were adopted carry the wound of wondering why we were given away. Those who stayed carry the wounds of living in a dysfunctional family with insecurity and trauma.

Is one type of wound worse than the other? I don't think so. They're different kinds of brokenness that require different paths to wholeness. Seeing my siblings' struggles has helped me understand that adoption, even with its primal wound, protected me from other, potentially worse wounds.

Your Journey: What Wholeness Really Means for Adoptees

Let's be honest: the world has some pretty unrealistic ideas about what it means to be "whole." Our culture's vision of a picture-perfect Christian life surely does not include mental health struggles. By the time they reach adulthood, adoptees are assumed to be "over" their adoption, know their complete history, and never feel triggered.

In reality, that's not how it works for adoptees. I'd like to insist that it is perfectly okay and understandable for wholeness to look different. Wholeness for those who have been adopted means that we:

- Manage our struggles instead of pretending they don't exist
- Make peace with questions that may never get answered
- Build good relationships, even when trust is hard
- Understand our triggers instead of being blindsided by them
- Accept that adoption is part of who we are, not something to get over

Why We Struggle More (And Why That's Normal)

When studies say adoptees have more mental health issues, people sometimes act like we're just weak. But the reality is that there are scientific reasons why our brains work differently.

Before we were even placed, we might have dealt with stress in the womb, birth trauma, or genetic predispositions. Then came the primal wound of losing our first mother, the confusion about identity, and feeling different from everyone around us.

After placement, we faced attachment challenges, family secrets about our adoption, and living without people who looked like us. Add in society's constant questions about our "real" parents, and you've got a recipe for struggle.

We're not broken. We're normal people who had abnormal beginnings.

What Wholeness Actually Looks Like

Sometimes wholeness includes taking medication every day. Sometimes it means regular therapy appointments. Sometimes it means accepting that certain questions will never be answered or that some relationships can't be fixed.

Wholeness isn't perfection. It's integration. It's not having no struggles; it's handling your struggles with grace and the right support.

Reflection Moment

As you take time alone to consider the ideas in this chapter about reaching wholeness, you may be working with new concepts and changing your way of thinking. These are the challenges I suggest for reflection and journaling.

1. Stop pretending it doesn't hurt. Adoption involves loss. Admitting this doesn't make you ungrateful for the situation you were placed into. Take a moment to feel the hurt.

2. Find help that empathizes. Not every therapist understands adoption. Find one who knows about the primal wound and doesn't try to talk you out of your feelings.

3. Build your toolbox. What works for you? Try different strategies. Some options that I have found helpful in the past include: therapy, medication, prayer, support groups, exercise—use whatever helps.

4. If possible, look at family patterns. Like the depression and suicide in my biological family, many adoptees inherit mental health struggles. Especially if you know this information, stay alert and get help early.

5. Change your story. Instead of "broken adoptee," call yourself "wounded and healed." Look for the ways God has used the circumstances of your life to create you, a beautiful and whole child of His.

Significant Next Steps

Ask yourself: What would wholeness look like for your specific situation? This might be different from what others expect. Think about the many areas of your life and how wholeness would impact each one. Your relationship with your family, your friends, your work, God, your memories. Take each one in turn and consider it. Then start building toward this vision of yourself as whole. Allow yourself to accept the place you're in and how God has made you.

Most importantly, remember this: You're not too much. You're not ungrateful. You're not broken. You're an adoptee on a journey toward wholeness, and that journey is important, life-giving work.

Prayer

Dear God,

You know every broken place in me—the ones I show the world and the ones I hide. I understand that wholeness in You doesn't mean having no struggles. Thank You that You use broken people, that Your power is made perfect in weakness, that You're close to the brokenhearted.

Give me understanding to see myself through your eyes, which are loving even while knowing all that I've been through. Help me see that my struggles don't disqualify me from Your purposes—they may even be part of them.

I claim Your promise that You make all things new. Help me be the generation where destructive patterns stop. Use my healing to help others heal.

Amen.

A Final Thought

My sisters Ardith and Lynne never got to experience complete wholeness on this earth. Their struggles overwhelmed them. But their lives were not failures. Ardith's advocacy helped countless others with mental illness. Lynne's story, though I know little of it, mattered. Their struggles are part of my story, pushing me toward my own healing and helping me help others.

My son Tommy found a different kind of wholeness—not the kind I'd hoped for, but perhaps the only kind available to him. His life taught me that sometimes we must accept wholeness that looks different than we imagined.

There's no one way to be whole. There's no perfect healing. Every adoption story has some scar tissue. It's a choice to look at the scars and know they mean we've survived and we're healing. The scars we carry give us the ability to help others on their journey.

Your journey to wholeness might include seeking therapy. It might also mean medication. No matter how much energy you put toward a search and reconciliation, your questions might not get answered, and relationships might not become healed. That's okay. God uses all types of circumstances to heal, and He loves us deeply as we are.

Dealing with Tough Times

When Love Isn't Enough

EVERY ADOPTIVE PARENT knows the moment. That crushing realization when you understand that all your love, all your trying, all your prayers might not be enough to heal your child. Every adoptee knows it too—that moment when you realize love can't erase the primal wound, can't fill every gap, can't answer every question.

If love is all that we need, what happens when love meets trauma? When hope meets mental illness? When dreams meet the harsh reality of attachment disorders, addiction, or behaviors that threaten to tear your family apart?

I thought I understood tough times. I'd survived my mother's suicide attempts. I'd navigated a divorce that made me a single mom. I'd worked through my own adoption issues in therapy. But nothing—nothing—prepared me for the kind of tough times that come when you adopt a child whose early trauma runs deeper than your love can reach. Or when your biological child, affected by the chaos of family dysfunction, loses himself to addiction.

Because I've faced them myself, I know tough times are so real. That's why we need to talk about the hard times that no one warns you about. The ones that don't have happy endings tied up with pretty bows. The ones where you have to choose between your sanity and your child. The ones where letting go is the most loving thing you can do. The ones where you question everything you thought you knew about family, faith, and the power of love.

I've learned that God doesn't promise us an easy life. What He does promise is sufficient grace, which Paul reminds us of in 2 Corinthians 12:9: "My grace is sufficient for you, for my power is made perfect in weakness." Sometimes that grace looks like healthy boundaries. Other times it looks like letting go. It may even look like accepting that the child you love may never be able to receive that love in the way you long to give it.

Let me tell you about the two boys who taught me that love is not always enough—but that "not enough" doesn't mean "worthless." It just means love sometimes has to take forms we never imagined.

My Journey: Two Sons, Two Battles, Too Much

Project CAN

Because my ex-husband and I were both adopted at birth, we had always planned to adopt a child. One day, while driving to work, I heard a commercial on the radio about Project CAN (Children with Adoptive Needs), so I called for information. The agency was supported by United Way, and they found homes for hard-to-place children, those who were handicapped, bi-racial, or part of sibling groups.

The social worker who interviewed us had never encountered adoptive parents who themselves were adopted, so this was new territory for her. After completing the necessary paperwork, classes, and interviews, all we could do was pray and wait to hear from them when they had a child.

I remember the classes vividly. They tried to prepare us for the challenges of adopting older children or those with special needs. We watched videos, learned statistics, and had adoptive parents share their stories—both the successes and the failures. Through all of that I sat there thinking, "That won't be us. We understand adoption. We've lived it. We'll know how to help a child who's been through trauma."

How naive I was. How arrogant, really, to think that because I'd been adopted as an infant into a loving home, I understood what a child who'd been abused and neglected for one and a half years might need.

When the call finally came, we went to their office full of excitement.

Tommy's Arrival

I've described Tommy and some of his struggles before, but here I want to focus on when he first joined our family. The agency offered us a little deaf boy who was three years old. As a reminder, he had been abused and neglected by his birth parents and placed into foster care when he was one and a half years old. Tommy's birth father had recently signed over his parental rights so his son could be adopted.

We said we would take him. However, we didn't know at the time that the agency had also offered him to another couple. Even though we wanted to take Tommy, the agency decided to place him with the other couple, because they had been waiting longer than we had. We were so disappointed, because we truly felt this child was supposed to be with us.

A few weeks passed and the agency called again to say that the other couple had just learned they were pregnant, so they turned down taking Tommy. Totally stunned, we figured that God did have plans for Tommy to be our child. In order to have him, we needed to quickly finish up everything required to complete the placement. I described earlier that this is when we had the opportunity to take Tommy from the foster home for the weekend for something like a trial run. After those couple of days, we had to take him back to the foster home for a few days before bringing him home for good.

I'll never forget that first weekend. Tommy was a beautiful little boy with red hair and bright blue eyes. But there was something unsettling about how easily he came with us. He didn't cry for his foster mom and had no stranger anxiety. He just...came. Like it didn't matter who he was with.

The social worker had said this was good—he was "adaptable." I learned later this was actually a red flag. Children who have had multiple caregivers often lose the ability to discriminate. Everyone is the same to them because they've learned that people come and go. They've learned that attachment is dangerous, so they don't do it.

Challenges

From the beginning, Tommy presented us with a variety of challenges and opportunities. Suddenly, we were parents of a deaf three-year-old who wore hearing aids in a pouch on his chest. We had to quickly learn sign language and started studying the method of Total Communication, which was used for educating deaf children. It combined sign language with lip reading and vocalizing words. We learned that we had to be assertive to be sure our son received an adequate education as guaranteed by federal law. All of this created a huge learning curve. We relied on the teachers at school and the social worker from the agency for guidance through everything. Tom was a handful, but we were so in love with this little boy with sparkling eyes and a wonderful smile.

As I earlier described, Tommy's bad behavior started with small things. Tantrums that lasted longer than typical. Destroying toys, especially ones he'd seemed to love. Lying about things that didn't matter. The social worker assured us this was normal for a child with his background. "Love and consistency," she said. "That's what he needs."

So we loved. And we were consistent. And the behaviors got worse.

About six months after adopting Tommy, I learned I was pregnant, and in August of 1978, my youngest son was born. Our family felt complete with our two boys. They both grew like weeds, and their unique personalities developed over time. Tom had red hair and blue eyes, and our younger son had blonde hair and big blue eyes, just like mine. As he grew up, he picked up sign language quickly. Later he was able to be his brother's interpreter when needed.

At first, I thought having a biological child would help Tommy feel more secure. See? We're a forever family. You have a brother. You belong. But instead, his arrival seemed to trigger something in Tommy. The negative behaviors escalated. I didn't learn until many years later that Tommy would hurt his brother when he thought we weren't looking. Not normal sibling stuff—calculated, cruel things.

How do you keep showing love to a child who seems determined to reject it? How do you protect your baby while trying to heal your older child? How do you not start resenting the chaos one child brings into your home?

Marriage Problems

During their childhood years, my marriage to my sons' father began to unravel. At one point we separated for a week but then reunited. Eventually my husband told me he didn't love me anymore, and after thirteen years of marriage, we separated. Counseling did not help. It was one of the most painful and difficult times in my life. I never imagined my marriage would fall apart. After a one-year separation, I filed for divorce.

I don't blame Tommy for our divorce, but the stress of dealing with his behaviors certainly didn't help. We were exhausted and spent so much money on therapists, special schools, and interventions, leaving no time for each other. All of our conversations were about Tommy's latest crisis. We forgot how to be husband and wife—we were just crisis managers.

As one counselor told me, God never planned for children to be raised by only one parent. My life as a single mom was stressful and exhausting. During this time, I decided to place Tommy at the Florida School for the Deaf and Blind (FSDB) in St. Augustine, which was almost a four-hour drive from our home. That's where he attended for grades seven and eight, coming home to visit once a month.

That decision to send Tommy away to school was excruciating. I felt like a failure. What kind of mother sends her child away? But he was becoming increasingly difficult to handle. His brother was terrified of him. I was terrified of him. The school for the deaf had resources we didn't—twenty-four-hour supervision, specialized therapy, peers who understood his world.

The weekend visits were actually pleasant. With the structure and support of the school, Tommy could hold it together for two days. We'd have glimpses of the son we'd hoped for—laughing, playing games, being part of the family. Then Sunday night would come, and he'd go back to school, and we'd all exhale.

And still, even his time at FSDB was challenging. He lived in a dorm with other boys and limited supervision. In those two years, Tommy managed to get suspended more than once before returning home and entering public school in ninth grade.

The Breaking Point

I can now see that Tom's behavior and mental health problems were probably related to a variety of issues. Unlike other deaf males, he did not have any learning disabilities, which was a plus. During his admission process, the psychologist at FSDB tested his intelligence and was surprised to report that he had a high IQ, enough to place him in the gifted range. Tom's ability to learn things quickly made school boring for him, and he constantly needed to be challenged.

I've described some of his behavior problems and run-ins with law enforcement. When he stole his father's car and wrecked it, that led to a six-week stay in a psychiatric hospital the summer before his senior year of high school. As I left the hospital, the tears streamed down my face, and I felt hopeless leaving my son locked up in that facility. His father and I knew it was necessary, but it frightened me on so many levels.

That psychiatric hospitalization forced me to finally face the truth: Love wasn't going to be enough.

All the adoption books talked about how adopted children just needed to learn to trust, to attach, to believe in permanency. They made it sound like a math equation: trauma + love × time = healing. Something was left out of this equation. It didn't consider that trauma experienced before a brain can form attachments may negate its ability to do so properly. His neural pathways were set before we ever met him. I needed to accept that some wounds may be too deep for family love to heal.

Without my faith, much prayer, and support from others, I would never have survived this painful, difficult season with Tom. After his summer in the psychiatric ward, he was to attend a vocational program for his senior year. He attended the school for just three weeks before running away. His choice to run away forced me to follow the terms of a contract with Tommy that I'd hoped would never be necessary.

This contract, which I've mentioned in a previous chapter, was one that Tom, his dad, and I created with his clinical psychologist. We all agreed on the rules and consequences and signed the contract. With this in place, Tommy knew ahead of time what would happen if he broke the rules.

When Tommy resurfaced after running away, I had to tell him that because of the contract and the terms we agreed to, which had now been violated, he could no longer live with me. Tough love is hard. Very hard. From the outside, not allowing him to live in my home looked heartless and brutal. I will tell you that it broke my heart. Even though I valued setting healthy, strong boundaries, I never wanted to use them.

I'll never forget that conversation. Tommy stood in my living room, defiant as always, sure I would cave like I had so many times before.

"You can't live here anymore," I said, my voice shaking. "We agreed. You knew the rules, and you signed the contract. You chose this."

"You're kicking out your own son?" he signed, his movements sharp with anger.

"I'm following through on what we all agreed to," I signed back. "I love you, but I can't allow you to live here and break the rules."

"You never loved me anyway," he signed.

And there it was. The wound that no amount of love could heal. My son's belief, buried so deep, but so real and raw, that he was unlovable, that he would always be second choice, that we would eventually abandon him like everyone else had.

"Your dad and I have loved you every single day since you came home with us," I signed through tears. "But love doesn't mean no boundaries. Love means wanting what's best for you, even when it's hard."

He left. And he never really came back.

Tommy's Struggle

When Tommy's father and I adopted him, we thought that love could overcome anything. We tried, and I believe we made a difference in Tom's life, but the reality is that his adoption didn't end up the way we had hoped. Overcoming serious mental health and behavior problems requires much more than love. Even with all the hours and money spent over the years on counseling, Tom was not able to function normally. His father and I did the best we could. Of course we made mistakes, and I'm sorry that all we did wasn't enough.

I had Tommy for fifteen years, and after that he traveled around living like a gypsy, gravitating to deaf communities in various states. From what we know, his birth parents had lived the same way, traveling up and down the eastern seaboard for years. Tom fathered two children with a common law wife, but they were unable to care for them adequately. Two aunts on their mother's side of the family adopted and raised the children. After sporadic contact through years of estrangement, sadly Tom passed away from lung cancer in August of 2022. His memorial service was attended by several deaf friends, as well as his daughter Tammy and her adoptive parents. He was finally at peace.

A Second Son

We named our second son after his grandfather. This felt appropriate, since he was born on his grandfather's birthday. I promise it certainly wasn't planned that way, because I was two weeks late and very pregnant. He was a delightful child, with that tow head of light blonde hair and huge blue eyes he inherited from me. As much as I loved Tom when we adopted him, giving birth to a child made me understand much more about our heavenly

Father's love for us. A love that led him to give us his only son, Jesus.

As a little boy, he had the sweetest spirit, and he could also be mischievous to a level that would reduce you to laughter and tears. He loved Cub Scouts, school, reading, art, comic books, and skateboarding.

But living with Tommy's chaos took its toll on him. He was hypervigilant, always watching for the next explosion or crisis. Sometimes our house may have felt volatile, and that led him to learn to be invisible, to not need too much, to not cause problems. He was the "good" child, the easy one. I admit his good behavior made me grateful at the time, but I am saddened that I didn't realize the ways in which he was disappearing into himself. Being "good" was his survival strategy.

Sadly, the divorce and other difficult issues he had with his brother took a severe toll on him. Behavior problems began, both at school and at home, and I started taking him to see the same psychologist Tom had seen. One day his assistant principal at middle school called to say he was being suspended for being in possession of marijuana. Sometime later we realized that pot was his gateway drug. When my son was suspended at age thirteen, his psychologist suggested that he go live with his dad.

The irony wasn't lost on me. I'd had to send Tommy away because of his behavior. Now it was recommended that I send my second son away for his behavior issues. But the reasons were so different. Tommy couldn't attach; my second son was too attached. Tommy acted out his pain through violence; his younger brother numbed his through substances. Same family, same chaos, completely different responses.

Alone

For the first time in my life, I was living alone. When I got married in 1972, I was eighteen and had gone from living with my parents to being married. Being alone was a huge adjustment, but I kept busy with work and church. My son's drug addiction eventually led to an arrest. His social worker at Juvenile Detention shared with me that he had experimented with a large variety of drugs. She told me it was a miracle he was alive.

The guilt suffocated me. How had I failed both my sons so completely? One couldn't live with me because of his violence. The other couldn't live with me because of his addiction. What kind of mother loses both of her children?

"You didn't lose them," my counselor told me. "You loved them enough to let them go where they could get help you couldn't provide. That's not failure. That's wisdom."

But it felt like failure. It felt like abandonment. It felt like I was doing to my sons what had been done to me—giving them away because I couldn't handle them.

With both of my children wayward, my best defense was prayer. The only way for me to cope with the battle of my son's addiction was to pray and trust God, knowing He was in control. I had done everything I could to get him the counseling and help he needed so badly. Sadly, one drug led to another. His arrests resulted in prison. My heart was absolutely broken. Why was all of this happening?

I remember visiting him in prison for the first time. My beautiful son looked hollow-eyed and lost.

"I'm sorry, Mom," he said through the glass. "I'm so sorry."

"I'm sorry too," I told him. "I'm sorry I couldn't protect you better. I'm sorry our home was so chaotic. I'm sorry you felt like drugs were your only escape."

I did the best I could, but had I? Had I really? Or had I been so focused on Tommy's dramatic needs that I'd missed my other son's quiet desperation?

It took several years, but over time he started to deal with his addiction, and his life slowly improved. He later married and eventually worked through his struggles in counseling and recovery. Today he is clean, sober, and has been married for eighteen years. He has his own business, which has become very successful, and he continues to heal every day. No matter what they've done, my unconditional love for both of my sons will never change.

Noel

My husband Noel has been a rock for me through the ups and downs and the heartbreak of my son's addiction. He brought three beautiful daughters (Heather, Michelle, and Melissa) to our blended family, and they have been a huge blessing in my life. These girls have given us seven beautiful grandchildren in addition to my son Tom's two children, for a total of nine wonderful grandchildren!

Noel came into my life when both boys were at their worst. He knew what he was signing up for: a woman with two deeply troubled sons. He could have run. Instead, he stayed. Even when my son went through an outpatient treatment program, Noel joined me for weekly family nights at the hospital as we supported my son's recovery.

He never tried to be a father to my boys. They had a father. But he was steady, present, unchanging—everything their chaotic childhoods had lacked. When my son got out of prison, Noel was there. When we got word of Tommy's death, Noel was there for me while I cried for the son I'd lost long before he died.

Surviving Hard Times

I know that since this is a book about adoption, it may seem off track to talk about my youngest son, who wasn't adopted. I am also fully aware that hard times come to everyone, regardless of if there are any connections to adoption at all. For our family, we did carry a lot of lingering emotional trauma. Whether this affected our relationships and the ways we interacted with one another, only God knows. But I do know that when God adopts us as His own, He promises never to abandon us. In the middle of all of the pain I've experienced, God has loved me without fail.

Sometimes I look back and marvel that I survived such hard times. You may also be wondering how to walk through your own difficult situations. Maybe you are in a season that feels heavy and painful. Just this morning you may have been reduced to a puddle of tears, begging God to intervene and be merciful. I've said before that I believe God has a plan for each of us. Nothing, absolutely nothing, happens to us that He doesn't know about. Do I understand why these things have happened in my life? No, I don't, but I also believe that God can use hard things to make us stronger and to teach us lessons we need to learn.

I used to think surviving meant fixing. If I could just fix Tommy, fix my youngest son, fix our family—then I would survive. But I've learned that sometimes surviving means accepting what we cannot fix. Sometimes it means letting go. Sometimes it means changing my outlook to include realistic expectations and the actual capabilities of those I love.

God kept Tommy alive long enough to father beautiful children who found stable homes, and they are a gift. Even during the chaotic days, God provided glimpses of joy that we recognized as His presence. He showed me that love has many forms, including boundaries.

My youngest son has survived addiction, found recovery, and broken the cycle. God never stopped working in our relationship, which has survived the prison visits, the disappointments, the fear.

Whatever difficult times you have gone through or are going through, my hope is that this book will allow you to see how you too can survive those tough times. As adoptees, we may have additional, unique issues that come into play, and I believe we can work through them together.

Tough times require strong faith, a faith that sustains. My faith is the foundation of who I am. I often wonder how people who have no faith cope with what life brings. How do they live through a serious illness, addiction, divorce, death, financial problems, rebellious teens, and so on?

Our Spiritual Journey

Our Father God loves us. All we need to do is call out to Him, because He wants us to talk to him. There are no special words or prayers needed; just talk to Him like you would a good friend. You can start with just a few words, like, "God, please help me. If you are real, please make yourself known to me."

In chapter four, I discussed my spiritual journey and how I accepted the forgiveness Jesus offers. My hope is that if you have never accepted Jesus, you will start by reading God's Word to learn about Him. Take the time to just sit and be still and ask Him to speak to your heart. My promise to you is that if you will open your heart and mind, seeking God, He will meet you right where you are. You don't have to get all cleaned up. We can come to Him just as we are. He loves you, and He is sufficient for all your needs.

"But God demonstrates his own love for us in this: While we were still sinners, Christ died for us" (Romans 5:8).

Shared Experiences: Different Kinds of Tough Times

Jen & Nick: When Love Means Accepting Limitations

Jen's first marriage of five years ended when doctors determined she could not safely have a child due to various blood disorders. When she later met Nick, she made sure he understood she could not have children. Immediately after they married, they started their research on various adoption agencies.

They heard good things about Bethany Christian Services, which is based in Michigan but also had an office in Winter Garden, Florida. Once approved, it took about eight months before their son Nash joined their family. The total adoption process concluded in 2018 and took approximately two years.

Jen believes their adoption specialist from Bethany Christian prepared them well for becoming adoptive parents. The organization required letters of recommendation, fingerprinting for a background check, home studies, and interviews. Theirs was an open adoption.

The birth mother, Kathy, had gone to an abortion clinic where she learned she was seventeen weeks pregnant. She was forty years old and already had three grown children. Outside of the clinic, she encountered a man who referred her to Choices Women's Clinic in Orlando. That's where she learned about all her options, made a birth plan, and chose adoption.

On her end of the process, Kathy was presented with profiles of three couples to choose from for her unborn child. Once he was born, the initial family Kathy had chosen for her son backed out after they learned he had Down syndrome. That's when Jen and Nick were offered the baby boy, and they said yes. They named him Nash and brought him home from the hospital when he was two days old.

"We knew immediately," Jen recalls when describing the process. "The social worker was so nervous telling us. 'The baby has been born, but there's something you need to know...' We could see her bracing for us to reject him too. But Nick and I looked at each other and knew. This was our son."

About a year prior to this moment, a friend had given Jen the book *The Lucky Few: Finding God's Best in the Most Unlikely Places* by Heather Avis. That book, which described Heather's story of adopting three children, two of which have Down syndrome, touched Jen's heart. Now that Nash has joined their family, Jen believes God used that book to prepare her and Nick in advance for the child that through adoption would one day be their son.

The couple speaks openly to their son about his adoption, even though he can't understand, and they talk about his birth mom, whom they call Auntie Kathy. One time the three of them met Kathy in person. She talked about Nash's diagnosis, concerned that she had passed it on to Nash. His condition had not been diagnosed while she was pregnant. Since Down syndrome is a genetic disorder, they reassured her there was nothing she could have done differently.

"That's part of our tough times," Nick explains. "Helping Kathy deal with her guilt. She thinks she caused his Down syndrome by considering abortion, by being stressed, by being older. We keep telling her it's not her fault, but she can't hear it. So we just love her through it."

Miraculously, in 2020, Jen gave birth to a daughter they named Harlowe. Family discussions of Nash's adoption have led their daughter to understand she stayed in her mother's belly, but that Nash was in someone else's belly.

The large Down syndrome community in central Florida has offered many opportunities to meet other similar families. Through the community's support, Jen and Nick have learned a lot about what to expect when raising a child with Down syndrome.

"Our tough times look different than most," Jen shares. "It's not behavioral issues or attachment problems. It's knowing Nash will never live independently. It's fighting for his education. It's dealing with people's stares and comments. It's grieving the life we imagined while celebrating the life we have."

Both Jen and Nick grew up in very narrow-minded, strict Baptist households, and their experience with adopting Nash and understanding his needs has not only been a blessing but has taught them to be more open-minded and sensitive to the struggles people face. Jen believes it has also taught their family to be more kind.

"We've had to redefine what success looks like," Nick adds. "Success isn't Nash going to college or getting married or having a career. Success is Nash learning to tie his shoes. Success is him saying 'I love you.' Success is his joy when he sees us. Success is smaller but so much sweeter."

Currently Nash is mainstreamed at an elementary school which previously had never had a child with Down syndrome. Jen and Nick have worked with teachers and administrators to provide their son with a good education, and teachers have been willing to take special training to meet Nash's needs. Jen and Nick continue to be advocates for their son Nash and for all children with Down syndrome. Their activism has had a ripple effect on all who meet them and their family.

If they were starting over, Jen said they would not go through an agency to adopt. Instead, they would foster or foster to adopt a child. They know couples who have fostered a child through the organization OneChild and have seen the positive impact this route can have on the child and their family.

"Not because we regret Nash," Jen quickly clarifies. "But because now we know our capacity. We know we can love a child with significant needs. We know we can handle tough times. And there are so many children in foster care who need families who understand that love doesn't fix everything, but it's still worth giving."

"The tough times aren't what we expected," Jen concludes. "We expected sleepless nights and tantrums. We got IEP meetings and therapy appointments. We expected him to grow out of difficulties. Instead, we grew into them. The tough times taught us that love isn't about fixing someone. It's about accepting them, limitations and all, and fighting for their best life possible."

∼

Your Journey: When Love Isn't Enough

We're told love conquers all. But what happens when love simply can't break through? This is a reality when trauma impacts and rewires a brain in the earliest years. That might look like attachment disorders that prevent healthy attachment from happening, no matter how intentionally we may work on a relationship. Love might not be enough when addiction, anger, and despair seem stronger than our capacity to love.

I've lived this. Love didn't fix my son's addiction or Tommy's anger. For years, I thought that meant I failed. But I have come to understand that what is needed in these times isn't more effort but a deeper understanding of what love looks like when we are in seasons of brokenness.

What Love Really Is

There are three things about love I've come to understand. Whether you are working through the reality of your adoption or loving an adopted child through difficult times, understand that God's love is unconditional, and that because of His love, we have the ability to love better than our natural tendencies lead us to think.

1. Love does not quit. That doesn't mean we don't make choices, like I had to make in setting boundaries with my boys, but we can make the conscious choice to choose to never stop loving the people in our lives.
2. Love sets boundaries. While we do not quit, God does not call us to be enablers but healers. That might look like saying "no" and establishing protection so healing can take place in safe places.
3. Love accepts reality. True love embraces people for who they are, not what we wish they were. God loves us in the middle of our messiness. He doesn't ask us to get cleaned up before we come to Him but looks at our situation and sees our heart, which is in need of love. Even the most difficult relationships involve human beings who are made in God's image with a capacity to love.

Reflection Moment

Have you ever faced a situation where love did not seem to be enough?

Maybe you have loved someone through addiction, anger, distance, rebellion, grief, or deep emotional pain. Maybe you have carried the quiet heartbreak of realizing that no matter how much you give, you cannot force healing, change, or peace.

Take a moment to reflect on these questions:

1. Where in my life am I trying to fix someone rather than love them wisely?
2. Have I confused love with rescuing, enabling, or ignoring reality?

3. What boundaries might be necessary for true healing to begin?

4. What pain, guilt, or disappointment do I need to place in God's hands today?

5. How might God be inviting me to trust Him in this difficult situation?

Sometimes the hardest truth is that love cannot control outcomes. But love can still remain faithful, prayerful, honest, and strong. As you reflect, ask God to show you what loving well looks like in your situation.

Significant Next Steps

When tough times come, it can feel overwhelming and isolating. You may feel as if you are the only one facing struggles that seem impossible to solve. While every situation is different, there are a few steps that can help you move forward with wisdom and faith.

Be honest about reality. Sometimes we spend years hoping things will change if we just try harder. Loving someone does not mean pretending problems are smaller than they are. Allow yourself to acknowledge the truth of your situation without shame.

Seek wise support. No one is meant to carry difficult burdens alone. Counselors, pastors, trusted friends, and support groups can provide perspective and encouragement. Reaching out for help is not weakness. It is wisdom.

Establish healthy boundaries. Boundaries are not punishment. They are protection. They create space where healing is possible and where love can exist without being consumed by chaos.

Release what you cannot control. One of the hardest lessons is accepting that you cannot fix another person's choices.

You can love, pray, guide, and support, but ultimately each person must choose their own path.

Anchor yourself in faith. During the hardest seasons of my life, prayer was the one place I could bring my pain honestly before God. He already knows your fears, doubts, and heartbreak. When everything else feels uncertain, His presence remains steady.

You may not be able to change every outcome, but you can choose how you respond. Choosing faith, wisdom, and love—especially when life is difficult—is a powerful step forward.

Finding God in the Mess

For a long time, I believed God's grace meant things would work out if I prayed and loved enough. But grace isn't about outcomes—it's about presence.

Sometimes grace is just enough strength for today.

Sometimes it's the courage to draw a hard line.

Sometimes it's peace in an imperfect story.

Even Jesus had a disciple who betrayed Him. Even David had a son who rebelled. Godly parents can still have children who make painful choices. That doesn't make you a bad parent. It makes you human in a broken world.

Prayer

Dear God,

Thank You that Your love isn't dependent on anything. Thank You that You don't measure our worth by what the world labels as success. You are present in the middle of every single crisis, and Your love never fails.

I ask for wisdom to know when to hold on and when to let go. Empower me with strength to love like You do. I understand that sometimes love requires boundaries and acceptance. Please guide me through each unique situation.

I trust You with my tough times, knowing You're acquainted with grief, familiar with rejection, experienced in loving those who push You away. Fill me with Your love, a love that never fails.

Amen.

A Final Thought

I used to think the tough times were a detour from the life God intended for us. Now I understand they ARE the life God intended—not because He's cruel, but because He knew we were strong enough, faithful enough, or simply available enough to love those who are hard to love.

Your tough times may look different. If you're on a journey to reconcile relationships with biological family members, reality may be different from what you had hoped it could be. If you're raising a child you've adopted, your struggles may be severe or less visible. Each family relationship is different. You may never reach a breaking point, or you might find yourself in the middle of a crisis right now.

My hope is to encourage you as you work to restore and reconcile relationships, or simply hold together ones that appear to be breaking apart. Please remember that you are not failing because it's hard. You are not weak because you're tired. You are not a bad child or a bad parent because love isn't enough.

You are brave. You are faithful. You are doing the sacred work of loving through difficult times. In God's economy, that kind of love—the kind that presses on when it's hard, that hopes when it's hopeless, that lets go when holding on would hurt more—that kind of love never returns void.

To Search or Not to Search?

IT STARTS AS A WHISPER. Maybe when you're filling out medical forms and have to write "unknown" for the hundredth time. Maybe when someone says you have your mother's eyes, and you wonder whose eyes you actually have. Maybe when your own child is born and you search their face for features you've never seen in a mirror.

The whisper becomes a question: Should I search?

For some adoptees, the answer is an immediate yes—a burning need to know that never goes away. For others, it's an absolute no—a door better left closed. But for most of us, it's a "maybe" that shifts with seasons, circumstances, and courage. A "maybe" that carries equal parts hope and terror.

What will I find? What if they're dead? What if they're alive but want nothing to do with me? What if they're wonderful? What if they're terrible? What if knowing is worse than not knowing? What if I'm betraying my adoptive parents? What if I'm betraying myself by not looking?

Underneath all these questions lies the deeper one: Who am

I, really? Am I who my adoptive parents raised me to be? Am I who my birth parents' genes say I should be? Or am I someone else entirely—formed by both nature and nurture, by questions and answers, by loss and love?

Let's talk about the search. On the surface it's a desire to find out the names and faces of our birth families, but ultimately it's a search for truth. What we're really looking for isn't just identities and medical histories. We're searching for the pieces of ourselves we've never seen, the story that began before our memory. It's a risk, because the truth we want to uncover might finally make us whole—or might shatter us completely.

But here's what I've learned: The truth, whatever it is, is better than wondering. What we find may be devastating, it may be beautiful. But the fact is that beautiful truth may bring us great joy while also introducing complications. Devastating truth may be difficult, but God makes us stronger and wiser as we grow in understanding. Sometimes, the search itself teaches us more about who we are than whatever outcome we might discover.

My Journey: From Forbidden Topic to Found Family

Despite the difficulties that I've encountered, the one thing that carried me through them has been my faith and relationship with Jesus. When I wasn't sure I could face an obstacle, and there were many, I found He was there to carry me through the tough times.

Jeremiah 29:11 says, "'For I know the plans I have for you,' declares the Lord, 'plans to prosper you and not to harm you, plans to give you hope and a future.'"

God's plans for me have been perfect because He is perfect. He always wants what is best for us. Nothing happens to us that isn't filtered through His hands. Circumstances in your life may not have been easy either. But I want you to know that God truly is in control, and He wants to assure you of His never-ending love for you. That special love abides within my heart, mind, and soul. God is good all the time.

As we piece together the stories that become the framework of our birth families, sometimes the information we learn is tragic. I found it helpful to think about what might have taken place if I hadn't been adopted. These pieces of the puzzle explain our life stories. Sometimes we choose to embrace our stories, and sometimes we decide instead to disregard what we have learned. We all have a choice. In my case, I felt a need to gather as much information as possible to understand my complete story.

When I was a child, my best friend Debbie told me I was adopted. When I asked my mom about my adoption, I learned quickly by her reaction that this was a forbidden topic in our house. Not because my mom was cruel, but because she was protective. I could see the fear in my mother's eyes when I first asked about it. I didn't know what that fear meant when I was young, but I can imagine some of her thoughts now.

She may have had fear that I would love her less. Fear that I would leave her for someone else. Fear that she wasn't enough. I remember her crying and asking why I was doing this to her. I was only ten, but I made a decision to never, ever bring up my adoption again. I learned to swallow my questions, to ignore the wondering, to pretend I didn't care about the woman who gave me away or the man who helped create me. I became the grateful adoptee, the one who didn't need to know, the one who was completely satisfied with the family I had.

But the questions didn't go away. They just went underground, surfacing at unexpected moments—in doctors' offices, in pregnancy, in the mirror when I wondered where my features came from. Eventually, I had to search.

The Letter That Changed Everything

It was way too easy, and it absolutely made no sense how I obtained my adoption records. Apparently, all I had to do was ask. The letter came from the judge's office in Clearwater. As I ripped open the envelope, my hands trembled with anticipation. Shockingly, the judge had granted my request to view my sealed adoption record. How astonishing that after all these years, all I had to do was ask, and my records would be unsealed. Suddenly I felt powerful, knowing that I would soon have access to the details of my adoption. I had conquered the legal system of the State of Florida. No one else was in control anymore. It felt wonderful to be so strong and in control, like winning the lottery.

I remember staring at that letter, my hands shaking. I'd written to the judge on a whim, really, never expecting a response. Previously I'd heard that Florida's adoption records were sealed forever, so I'd prepared myself for rejection. Instead, I held permission—permission to know, permission to look, permission to find the truth that had been unknown for thirty-seven years.

But with the permission came fear. What if my adoptive mother and stepfather found out? They were still alive then, and I knew my search and discovery would wound my mother. I told myself I was protecting her by keeping it secret, but really, I was protecting myself from her pain, her questions, and her fear that she would lose me.

My Adoption Record

As soon as possible, I drove to the courthouse in Clearwater. After presenting my letter from the judge to the Clerk of the Court's office, I sat down in front of a bulky microfiche machine to view my birth records from 1954. There it was, the name of my birth mother. The woman who had given birth to me in Dunedin at Mease Hospital was Margaret Matilda Agnew, whose maiden name was Clark. My birth father was not listed on my birth certificate, and to this day I still do not know his identity.

Margaret. Maggie. Such an ordinary name for the woman who had haunted my dreams. I'd imagined her in every way possible—young and scared, old and bitter, beautiful, plain, rich, poor, desperate, indifferent. But she was just Margaret. A woman with a middle name and a maiden name and a story I didn't yet know.

The absence of my birth father's name felt like another rejection. Not important enough to name. Not involved enough to claim me. Just blank space where half my heritage should be.

I searched further for other public records at the courthouse, discovering legal documents including Margaret's marriage license, a divorce, a remarriage, and then a second divorce from her husband Robert. Divorce papers listed their four children. That meant I had siblings! Suddenly, in a split second, I learned I was not an only child.

There I was in 1991, at the age of thirty-seven, suddenly realizing I had two brothers and two sisters. Maybe my mouth hung open as I looked through the machine. I never dreamed I had siblings, so it felt like I stared through the glass at the document listing four names for hours. My brain felt frozen and could hardly process what I had read. I wanted to announce to the world, "Hey, I'm not an only child, I have siblings!" The documents showed all four of my older siblings had the same parents, Robert and Margaret Agnew.

Four siblings. Four people who shared my mother, who might look like me, sound like me, think like me. Four people who were kept and raised while I was given away. My joy of discovery quickly mixed with the pain of rejection. Why did she keep them and not me? What was wrong with me? Or what was wrong with the situation when I was born?

I made copies of my adoption records and the legal documents and left the courthouse. My feet practically floated as I walked back to my car. Wonder, fear, anxiousness, and excitement swirled around me.

On the drive to work from the courthouse, my mind spun like a merry-go-round out of control. Once at work, I went straight to my boss's office to tell him my big news. I felt giddy knowing I had finally found some of the missing pieces of my life. My boss, who had been supportive of my search, shared in my happiness.

If you can imagine, all of this took place before the internet even existed. That meant all of my research had been conducted by mail and phone. Along the way I discovered an organization called Adoptees' Liberty Movement Association (ALMA), which proved to be helpful. After my trip to the courthouse, I contacted them for advice. Even though I had the names of my siblings, I understood that since women often take their husband's last names when getting married, my sisters' names may have changed. Looking for my brothers would be easy, but finding my sisters would be more difficult.

Years of Waiting

I originally discovered the names of my birth family in 1991, when the judge granted me permission to see my adoption records. Even though I was longing to find out the information, it wasn't until I married Noel in 1995 and he encouraged me that I continued with the search. Even then, a long time passed as I sat on the information I had discovered at the courthouse. Around 2004, I read an article in my local newspaper about a licensed private investigator named Alvie Davidson. I decided to contact him, and he came to our home one evening to look at the records I had collected. While looking over the information, he told me I had already done all of the hard work.

Through his special access to numerous databases for licensed investigators, he had located my birth family by the next morning.

That made thirteen years of knowing names but not faces, knowing they existed but not where. Why did I wait? Fear, mostly. Fear of disrupting their lives. Fear of rejection. Fear of what I might find. Fear of losing the family I had by finding the family I'd lost.

But also, life. Divorce. Single parenting. During some seasons, I was just trying to survive, and the luxury of searching for my birth family felt selfish, indulgent, even impossible.

Noel changed that. "You deserve to know," he said simply. "Whatever you find, I'll be here. But you deserve to know your story."

The Phone Call That Changed Everything

The morning after Alvie came to our home, he called me at work. "I found them all," Alvie said. "Your siblings are all alive. Do you want me to make contact?"

When he told me he'd already found my relatives, it took my breath away. I was stunned not only because he had found them so fast, but because I now could have the knowledge of where my siblings and other family members were located.

Alvie went on to tell me that my birth mother and maternal grandmother were deceased, but I did have an Aunt Ardith, who lived about an hour and a half away in St. Petersburg. Her family included my numerous first and second cousins, and they also lived in the same geographic area. Alvie told me that my closest sibling was Amber, who lived in Tallahassee. My oldest brother, Robert, and my sister Ardith were living in Arizona, and my other brother, Tommy, was in Colorado.

I hadn't realized until that moment how much I'd feared everyone was dead, that I'd waited too long, that my chance for answers had passed. But my aunt and siblings were alive. Scattered across the country like seeds from a dandelion, but alive.

With my permission, Alvie acted as an intermediary and contacted my siblings to see about their interest in exchanging phone numbers with me. I'm sure I didn't get any work done that day and probably couldn't focus on much of anything else for the rest of the week. Along with my excitement, a bit of fear remained. A different fear now, wondering: What would happen next? Would my birth family accept or reject me?

While the information about my siblings thrilled me, the news that my birth mother was no longer living hit harder than I'd expected. Dead. No chance for answers from her. No opportunity to ask why she made the choices she did. No possibility of hearing "I'm sorry" or "I never forgot you" or even "I did what I thought was best." Just...gone.

First Contact

My first connection came by phone from my older brother, Tommy, followed a few minutes later by a call from my sister Amber. She and I quickly determined during our conversation that we shared similar interests, and we exchanged email addresses and promised to stay in touch, as we'd both asked one another a multitude of questions. Robert, the oldest sibling, asked me not to contact my sister Ardith due to her mental health issues. He served as her guardian and wanted to first consult her therapist before revealing my existence to her. After approval from her counselor, Robert did give her my phone number.

All of these conversations felt a little awkward. Suddenly I was having phone conversations with strangers who were family, speaking with voices that sounded a little like mine. Tommy was cautious. Amber was warm but perhaps a little worried. What did I want? Would I disrupt their lives?

"I just want to know where I come from," I told them. "I want to understand as much as possible."

What they told me in those early conversations began to paint a picture I hadn't expected. They gave a description of my birth mother, not as a young girl in trouble, but as a woman who had four children she could barely care for. A woman who struggled with depression. A woman married to a difficult man whose life was chaotic.

In those early days of conversing, Tommy and Amber contacted my Aunt Ardith, who happened to be out West on vacation. They gave me her cell number, and I called to introduce myself. I learned that she had known about me but had promised her sister to keep my existence confidential. I'm not sure why she felt the need to continue to keep me a secret after Maggie, her sister, my birth mother, passed away in 2001. After almost fifty years, the truth was out in the open.

"You were so lucky you were adopted!" Those were some of the first words my aunt said to me. Not "I'm sorry we kept you secret" or "We wondered about you" but "You were lucky."

At first that word stung. Lucky to be given away? Lucky to not know where I came from? Lucky to have this hole in my history? But as I learned more, I began to understand exactly what she meant.

Meeting Face to Face

Soon after, I heard from my first cousin, Ardie Ruth, Aunt Ardith's third child. She wanted to meet me face to face before anyone else did. I could hardly wait for the meeting to finally see a relative from my birth family. We met at the Macaroni Grill in Brandon, Florida for dinner. She greeted me warmly and showed me an entire packet she'd brought along, which had copies of family trees and photos. I learned my family heritage was Scottish, and Ardie Ruth confirmed this through her long, beautiful red hair, complimented by her sparkling green eyes. She had a vibrant personality and didn't miss a beat when describing the members of my birth family.

Looking at the photos was like looking at ghosts made flesh. Features I'd seen in the mirror suddenly made sense. Eyes shaped the same as mine stared back at me in my mother's photo. The curve of my smile echoed in my siblings' faces.

But more than a window into where I'd received my physical features, Ardie Ruth gave me insights into the story of my family. She shared her perspective on her Aunt Maggie's family, which she'd witnessed as it broke apart from dysfunction, mental illness, and poverty. She described children (my siblings) raising themselves. It was a story of survival against odds. Her insights confirmed what her mother had told me: My adoption wasn't a rejection, but a rescue into a better life.

The Aunt Who Told the Truth

When Aunt Ardith returned from her trip, we also met in person. Noel and I invited her and Norval, her companion, to come to our home in Lakeland for a Saturday lunch. I was thrilled to have the opportunity to meet them but wondered how I would be accepted. As I waited for them to arrive, I paced and worried. Finally, the doorbell rang. When I opened the door, my aunt said, "Oh my, you look more like Maggie than her real children do!" Then she stopped and said, "Oh, that's right, you are her real child!"

That moment encapsulated the complexity of adoption reunions. I was real but not real. Family but not family. Known but secret. Connected but separate.

My aunt shared endless stories over lunch. She also answered numerous questions from all of us. Not long after our first meeting, my husband and I were invited to my aunt's home for a family gathering, complete with all the first and second cousins. All four of my aunt's children were there: Bud, Thomas, Ardie Ruth, and Nancy. What a lively bunch they were, warmly welcoming us to the family. They didn't hesitate to accept me, this new relative who had just appeared out of nowhere.

But the stories my aunt told were hard to hear. Stories of my birth mother's struggles, her men, her inability to care for her children. Stories of neglect and abuse. Stories of my siblings' suffering. Stories that made me grateful for my boring, stable, loving adoptive home.

Finding More Pieces

Further research with the State of Florida led me to request and obtain a copy of the social worker's notes from the interview she'd conducted with my birth mother the month after I was born. Information from that interview painted a very difficult and somewhat disturbing picture.

The social worker's notes describing Maggie were clinical but devastating:

"Mother presents as overwhelmed and unable to cope with another child. States she has four children at home and cannot provide adequate care for another. When asked about the father, she became evasive and would only state he is not her husband and is not able to provide support. Mother appears relieved by adoption plan and shows no ambivalence about placement."

No ambivalence. Those words hurt more than they should have. I wanted to read that she struggled, that she cried, that she held me just once. Instead: no ambivalence.

It hurt my heart to process the mental and emotional state of my birth mother at the time when she let me go. While reading all of that brought me pain, those notes also brought a surprise. The social worker's notes revealed that I had a fifth sibling, another sister, who had also been given up for adoption at birth.

She had been born two years before me. I later learned her name was Lynne Hope.

The Harsh Reality

As a summary, this is what I knew: Bob and Maggie had their first two children, Robert and Ardith, in 1945 and 1946. They divorced and later remarried in 1948, and had two more children, Tommy and Amber, in 1949 and 1950. In 1951, Maggie and Bob divorced for the second time. Lynne was born in 1952 and placed for adoption, and I was born in 1954. Both Maggie and Bob remarried in 1955, just days apart. That's when Maggie married Shepard Rosenberg and Bob married Iva Ball.

This timeline tells a story of chaos. Children born into an unstable marriage. Divorce and remarriage to the same person. More children. Another divorce. Remarriages. And through all of this, children grew up without the stability they needed.

Even though my father's name was not listed on my birth certificate, I didn't give up hope of finding my birth father, and I completed DNA testing. Because of Maggie's on-again, off-again relationship with Bob, I needed to first rule out whether or not he was my birth father. After completing DNA testing through Ancestry.com, I confirmed that Bob Agnew was not my birth father. Some of my siblings have also completed DNA testing. Of those who have, my sister Amber shares 26% of my DNA, which would be correct for a sibling sharing the same birth mother. My niece, who is my brother Tommy's daughter, matches me at 13%.

Through this process, a mysterious relative emerged. The person with the next highest matching DNA at 24% is a probable half sibling on my unknown birth father's side. So I have another sibling somewhere out there. Someone who possibly shares my unknown father. Someone who might have answers about half my heritage. Realistically, another door that might never open.

Meeting Amber

I am grateful for all of my siblings whom I have had the opportunity to meet, but my closest sibling is my sister Amber, who lived about five hours away in Tallahassee when I met her. We made plans for her, along with her husband Dave and their daughter, to visit me in Lakeland. When we met for the first time, it was evident we clearly favored one another, sharing our birth mother's blue eyes. My niece and my youngest son share those big blue eyes as well.

Looking at Amber was like looking at an alternate version of myself. Externally, we had the same eyes and similar smiles. What I've come to understand is that she carries a burden I don't have. Because she was raised by the mother who gave me away, she lived the life I'd escaped.

Before meeting, one of the first photos Amber sent me was of our mother on her wedding day. It pictured Maggie, at just sixteen years old, marrying George Robert Agnew, who was an Army man whom everyone called Bob. Sixteen. A child bride. Set at such a young age on a path that would lead to six children, two given away, four damaged by their upbringing. The photo showed a pretty girl playing dress-up in a wedding gown, not ready for marriage, certainly not ready for motherhood.

Their wedding took place with her mother Grace's encouragement. What was Grandma Grace thinking? Did she think Maggie, even at the age of sixteen, would be better off married? I was told that Grandma Grace really liked Bob, and she was even listed as a witness of the marriage ceremony.

The Stories That Explained

Over time, numerous additional stories emerged from my birth family, especially from my aunt and siblings. One of the most difficult experiences for my siblings occurred in 1955, during the time when Maggie and Bob were divorced. That's when Bob temporarily moved to Texas with his four children and new wife. After living a month near Corpus Christi, he then proceeded to drop off his children at an orphanage.

An orphanage. My siblings that were not given away through adoption ended up in a home for children, with no parents, while I was safe in my adoptive home. The irony is painful. On the surface, it appears that those four were the "real" children, the kept ones, the ones who weren't given away. But in an even more traumatic way, they lived a life of being abandoned, traumatized, discarded.

Thankfully the Herald of Healing Children's Home was a Christian orphanage run by a pastor, and that gives me hope that the children were treated with love. I cannot begin to imagine how my siblings felt, to be abandoned so abruptly by their father. Emotions of fear and trauma must have been overwhelming. How does a parent do that to their children?

We aren't sure what led to his surrender of the children, but I speculate that his new wife wasn't interested in a ready-made family with four little mouths to feed. After my siblings lived in the orphanage for a year, the administrators contacted Bob to say he must pick up the children. If he didn't, his only other option was to sign over his parental rights so they could be adopted.

That ultimatum prompted Bob to pick up his children. Rather than a joyful reunion, with stories and tears of the past year, their father drove my siblings straight to Pensacola, Florida and dropped them off on Maggie's doorstep. At this point, my siblings ranged in age from Robert, who was twelve, to Amber, who was six. Ardith, eleven, and Tommy, seven, filled in the middle.

When Bob showed up with their children at his ex-wife's doorstop, he told her, "Now it's your turn!" As if children were possessions to be passed back and forth. As if their trauma didn't matter. As if they were problems to be managed, rather than children to be loved.

From that point my siblings lived with Maggie and her new husband, Shepard, in Pensacola, where Shepard worked on the naval base. When Robert turned eighteen, he joined the Air Force, probably to escape his difficult home life. As for Ardith, she reported the abuse she suffered at home from her mother to a school counselor, and this resulted in being removed from her home by the police on her sixteenth birthday. She was sent back to live with her father, Bob, who at that time was living in California.

Tommy also wanted to escape, so he lied about his age and joined the Navy. That left Amber at home. She lived with Maggie and Shepard until her eighteenth birthday, when Maggie handed her a suitcase and told her to start packing, because she was done with her and Amber wouldn't be living there any longer. The next day, Amber was on a bus headed to Tallahassee to live with Shepard's brother and his family. What awful feelings of rejection she endured after being suddenly kicked out of her home.

Each of my siblings left Maggie's abusive home on or before their eighteenth birthdays. The woman who was meant to provide love and shelter couldn't wait to give them away. Although my siblings weren't given away as infants like Lynne and I, our mother also rejected them, in perhaps a worse way, as they left her as damaged young adults who would carry her rejection forever.

The Truth About Being Lucky

As I've learned all of this and more about my birth family, I've come to believe that what my aunt said about me being the lucky one is one hundred percent true. Lynne and I both escaped the dysfunctional family life my siblings had to endure for years.

Thankfully we were both adopted, which I interpret to be God's way of protecting us.

My Aunt Ardith told me she tried on more than one occasion to talk her sister into letting the four children live with her. But for some reason, Maggie refused. Even though Maggie's own mental health problems prevented her from being the mother she needed to be, she refused to allow anyone else to care for her children. Not even her sister Ardith, who had the financial means to provide for them.

Did she think letting them go would make her look like a failure? Or maybe she thought others would view her as incapable if she received help caring for her children. Even though she wouldn't accept Ardith's help, her life must have been stressful. The court transcript of Maggie's second divorce from Bob states she had developed a stutter, caused by the stress and dysfunction of her marriage. Setting aside the beauty of bringing four children into the world with Bob, Maggie paid a high price for living in such a difficult environment. Bob had his own personal battles that also influenced the entire family.

It's clear that Maggie and Bob each struggled with mental health issues. I often wonder whether or not they received professional help, and if they didn't, could that have made any difference in their ability to take care of each other and their children?

The truth was complicated. My birth mother was both a wounded woman and the wounder of others. Even though I never met her, I think of her as a child bride who never grew up, who hurt her children in ways that reverberated through generations. But I also acknowledge her as a woman who perhaps knew her limitations when it came to Lynne and me. Her decision to give us away may have stemmed not from lack of love but from moments of clarity about what she could and couldn't provide.

"You were so lucky you were adopted!" My aunt's words

frequently echo in my mind. Yes. Yes, I was. Not lucky to lose my birth mother, not lucky to grow up with questions, not lucky to be different. But, lucky to escape. Lucky to be loved. Lucky to have a chance at a normal life.

Finding Peace with Truth

Those of us adoptees who have evaluated and acknowledged both the good and the bad that life has presented have a greater capacity to live a normal and well-balanced life. Even still, many adoptees find great help in receiving ongoing mental health services. Each situation is different; some of us need the help more frequently, and some will never need those services.

What I found in my search was not what I expected. It was a surprise to find answers that raised new questions. I'd dreamed of a reunion, of finally belonging somewhere, of filling the hole in my heart. Instead, I learned details of a story that made me grateful for the life I'd lived. At first my new found siblings were strangers. In recent years we've come to understand that even though we did not grow up together and had very different childhoods, we are connected by blood, and our relationships have great value.

Through my search, I've also found peace. Peace in knowing the story of my origin. Peace in understanding that my adoption was not rejection but God's protection. Peace in seeing God's hand in placing me exactly where I needed to be. Peace in the truth, however complicated it is.

Shared Experiences: Different Searches, Different Truths

Amber: The Sister Who Stayed

My sister Amber's stories of her childhood were hard to hear. She lived day in and day out with our mother Maggie's strong emotional highs and lows. Abuse and neglect were part of her reality. To survive, Amber had to lean on her older brother Robert for support.

"When Mom kicked me out on my eighteenth birthday, part of me was relieved," she admitted. "I was so tired of being afraid all the time. Tired of never being good enough."

At the same time, she loved Maggie, and being forced to leave someone she loved brought painful and complicated emotions. "She was still my mom," Amber said. "I kept hoping she'd change, that one day she'd be the mother we needed. She never did."

In order to make peace with our mother's failures, Amber came to understand her limitations. "She was broken," Amber said simply. "Broken people break people. But the cycle stops with us." Amber continued to reflect on being forced to move in with a new family. "You know what's funny?" Amber asked. "Maybe being kicked out was the best thing that ever happened to me. Shepard's brother and his wife were kind and willing to give me a place to live. Sometimes rejection is redirection."

Ardie Ruth: The Cousin Who Kept the Secret

I described earlier when I first met my cousin, Ardie Ruth. She had welcomed me warmly and brought me an entire packet with copies of family trees and photos. "I've known about you for a long time," she confessed.

Ardie Ruth had done her own searching, not because she

needed to find her birth family, but because she was curious about the truth in the family. She'd compiled genealogies, collected photos, and interviewed elderly relatives. Through this research, she became the family historian, the keeper of stories.

"I think secrets make families sick," she told me. "Your existence was a secret. Lynne's existence was a secret. The emotional and physical abuse Maggie participated in was a secret. With so many secrets, I decided I wanted to be the generation that told the truth."

At that first meeting, she showed me photos of our grandmother Grace, our great-grandparents, cousins I'd never known I had. Each photo came with a story, which sometimes involved dysfunction. "But we're survivors," Ardie Ruth said proudly. "Look at all of us. We survived. We broke cycles. We're doing better than the generation before us. And that's something."

Multiple Siblings' Perspectives on the Search

As I've pieced together my birth family's story, each of my siblings has had a different reaction to being found in my search and establishing our connection:

Robert (the oldest) remains distant. He answered my initial questions but made it clear he had no interest in building a relationship with me. I assume he survived his adult life by leaving it all behind, with no interest in revisiting the past. I respect his boundaries, his need to protect himself.

Ardith (my sister with bipolar disorder) was eager to connect but struggled with stability. Our relationship included long phone calls where she'd pour out memories, followed by several weeks of silence. She needed me to understand what I'd escaped. "You don't know how lucky you were," she'd say. Her suicide in 2022 meant we'd never fully resolve our relationship.

Tommy has been protective of the family, even the dysfunctional parts. Maybe he worried I'd judge them, that I'd think I was better because I'd been raised differently. That has never been my intent. My goal has been to understand what happened all those years ago in our family.

Amber became my closest sibling connection. Maybe because she'd found her own redemption. Maybe because she understood that families can be both broken and beautiful. She became my bridge to understanding the life I'd escaped. Our shared faith made our relationship even more special.

Finding Lynne's Shadow

It was a shock to discover the social worker's notes about my fifth sibling. She had been born two years before me, and I later learned her name was Lynne Hope.

Lynne remains a ghost in our family story. Through research, I learned:

- She was born in 1952.
- Her adopted mom was a nurse and her father a postman.
- She married several times.
- She struggled with depression her whole life.
- She died by suicide in North Carolina.

Through studying her obituary records, I learned of her sister-in-law and made contact with her. She revealed that Lynne had always felt incomplete. She'd died never knowing she had five siblings, never knowing she wasn't alone.

Lynne's story haunts me. We walked parallel paths of being adopted and enduring many struggles in life. In some ways I feel guilty that I found answers and she didn't. I survived and she didn't. If I didn't believe in God's hand in my life, I would only see randomness, unfairness, and tragedy. But instead, I believe God held me from the moment of my conception.

Your Journey: The Impact of Searching

When I embarked on the search for my birth family, I stepped out with little knowledge of what I was getting into. My husband encouraged me, and I was motivated to understand my history. With just a little ambition and support from Noel, I made tentative steps. One thing led to another, and I've entered deep into a larger understanding of the complications and peace that have come with the process. Here are a few insights I've learned about searching for your roots:

1. Be honest about what you want. Curiosity, closure, identity—whatever drives you is valid. Wanting to know your story does not mean you are rejecting your adoptive family.
2. Know the risks. Searching can bring joy, pain, or both. Be ready for silence, rejection, or unexpected truths alongside the hope of connection.
3. Get support. This is not something to do alone. Find an adoption-competent therapist, join a support group, and talk to others who have searched before.
4. DNA results and online tools make it easy to find people fast, but relationships take time. Let your emotions catch up to the facts.
5. Hold the tension. You can love your adoptive parents and still long to know your birth family. You can feel both grateful and angry. Both belong in your story.

Reflection Moment

As you consider whether now is the time to begin or continue the search for your birth family, prepare your heart for what you may find. The process and results are rarely simple. Some adoptees will find warmth and welcome from their birth families. Others will face distance, silence, or loss. Most often, it is a mix of all of this, a tension of joy and grief sitting side by side.

Be prepared to accept that while searching may appear on the outside to be about finding people, it's often about finding yourself. There will be a process to make peace with the family that raised you and the one that gave you life.

Maybe you've seen a Hallmark movie or read a book where the search for a birth family brings a blend of experiences, resulting in peace gained from questions answered and perfect outcomes. Often, peace is a work in progress where we accept what is. Some questions will not be answered. Some relationships will not heal. Even in this, the hard truth can bring freedom, because it ends the wondering.

Significant Next Steps

Before you take the next step toward finding your birth family, I encourage you to seriously consider the following questions:

- What do I truly hope to find? What have you imagined your birth family to be like? Do you hope your birth mother has always wanted to know about you? Would you be hurt if your birth parents have a healthy, happy family that doesn't include you?
- Am I emotionally ready for any answer? There are all kinds of scenarios that lead to adoption. What would happen if the reality is different from what you imagine?
- Who will walk with me if it hurts? Whatever answers you uncover, you'll want to process what you find. Maybe your adoptive family isn't supportive of your search. Maybe you worry it will hurt them if you express a desire to know. Share your plans with people around you who share your desire to know. Find

people who will be there for you to talk through the answers you uncover.

Finally, if you choose to search, go in with open hands and an open heart. Whatever you find, it can become part of your healing.

Prayer

Dear God,

You are truth. You know what I'll find if I search and what will remain hidden if I don't. You know the names I long to know, the faces I long to see, the stories I long to hear.

Give me wisdom to know whether or not to search. If I'm searching for something only You can provide, redirect my heart. If I decide to search, prepare me for what I'll find. Give me strength to handle rejection, wisdom to navigate dysfunction, grace to forgive what needs forgiving, and boundaries to protect what needs protecting.

Help me remember that my identity is not determined by what I find or don't find. I am not defined by who kept me or who gave me away. I am defined by You—the One who has always known me, always wanted me, always claimed me.

Thank You that no search can change Your love for me. Help me find my ultimate identity in You—the One who knows me completely.

Amen.

A Final Thought

My search revealed difficult truths. I learned that my birth mother was broken and my siblings were damaged. It grieves me that my birth father remains unknown.

But I'm glad I searched.

Not because it was easy or beautiful or healing in the way I'd hoped. But because even the difficult truth is better than wondering. Understanding my origins has helped me understand myself, and by seeing what I escaped, I am exceedingly grateful for what I received. Your search may yield different results. Like me, you might find open arms, or there might be only closed doors. You might find answers or more questions.

And whether your birth family is found or lost, functional or broken, welcoming or rejecting, you belong. You belong to the family that raised you. You belong to the family that gave you life. Most importantly, you belong to the God who orchestrated it all.

Some of us need to search. Some of us need to not search. Both are valid choices. Both require courage. Both can lead to peace.

The question isn't whether to search or not. The question is: What do you need for your own journey toward wholeness? Will it be better to know the answers, whatever they might be? Or would your heart be more whole by coming to the acceptance that you don't need or want to know?

The decision is yours to make.

And we know that in all things God works for the good of those who love him, who have been called according to his purpose.

ROMANS 8:28

After the Search, After the Healing: What Now?

WE'VE OPENED UP, looked at, and discussed many aspects surrounding adoption. At this point, I hope you've taken time for honest reflection and faced the adoption wounds you're carrying. Hopefully, you've also made peace in deciding whether to search or to make peace without knowing all of the details. These are all key steps in moving from brokenness toward wholeness.

You may be wondering what the next steps are after coming to acceptance of your adoption. Do adoption stories simply end with being healed and whole, living happily ever after? Or is this where your real story and purpose begins?

Here is what I have discovered, and this principle applies to people who endure traumas of all kinds. Once someone makes it to a place of healing after any sort of difficult experience, they carry something precious, which is the ability to help others navigate the same dark waters they have crossed. This applies to you no matter if you chose to find your birth family or not, and regardless of the outcome if you did search. If you've walked through these emotions, you have the ability to transform pain into purpose.

It's on the other side of pain that we become wounded healers, guides for those still working through the process.

I'm Glad I Was Adopted

If you'd asked me at seven, I would have said I was not okay with being adopted.

The sting remained when I was eighteen and answering "unknown" for the hundredth time on medical forms asking about information on my family medical history. Each answer reminded me that I didn't know where I came from.

Then, at thirty-six, when I turned the knob on the microfiche and discovered I had siblings who were kept, I couldn't make sense of why I was the expendable one.

At fifty, when I met my birth family and learned about the dysfunction I'd escaped, I would have said I was lucky—but lucky isn't the same as glad.

But now, at seventy-one, I can truly say, "I'm glad I was adopted."

It's not just that I've made peace with being adopted. I am genuinely, deeply, and profoundly glad.

The Journey to Glad

My journey to gladness didn't come easily or quickly. I've detailed the journey here in this book, but this is my main point.

This journey to wholeness in my adoption story has been intentional and has come through hard work.

In counseling, I've worked through this primal wound. Often many tears were shed in Betty's office, but I have come to embrace that being adopted is something to grieve AND celebrate. I grieve the truth I discovered when I learned that my sister and I had been given away, and at the same time, four of my siblings endured great trauma by being kept.

Even though I never met my birth mother, I came to understand her brokenness. God gave me courage to extend grace to the decisions she made as I believe she tried to do the best she could with the little that she had.

The love of my adoptive parents who desperately wanted me plays a key part in my journey. They gave me opportunity and a family when my biological parents could not. Not only did they meet my needs, but they became a representation of the way God has adopted me into His family. Ultimately, God gives my story purpose and makes it clear that He has been near from the moment of my conception.

God also has redeemed my journey by bringing opportunities to share my story with other adoptees looking for their purpose. My story isn't random, and neither is yours.

What Gladness Does Mean

To better understand what I mean by using the word glad, I need to clarify that this place of contentment doesn't take away the questions and understanding I carry about my past.

I will always wonder who my birth father was, and I still grieve that I never had a connection with my birth mother. Adoption is beautiful, but it is messy. Earlier in this book, you read of the complicated emotions that the adoptees I interviewed shared. Those are emotions I've experienced as well, and I've shared about the trauma in my life and my sons'.

Trauma is inevitable when a child is given away to another family, and the dysfunction this all brings does need to be addressed.

But God.

There is no mess or trauma God can not work through and redeem. The pieces may not all get put back together the way we think they should, but we can trust that God never stops working. He was there in that delivery room when I entered the world. He prepared my birth mother to release me and my adoptive mother and father to receive me.

Even in that loss, God protected my life and put me in a place of being chosen. He chose me from before the world began, and He prepared my parents to make the choice to love me, which they did again and again.

Because of all of these things, I can help others in ways I never could have if my story were simpler. I also understand the value of belonging to a larger company that includes millions of adoptees throughout history, including Jesus Himself.

Finding Purpose in the Pain

Since being retired, I've been amazed at how often God has placed people in my path who are working through their experiences with adoption. Most of them have different needs, but we all have one Lord. I see on a regular basis that by making myself available, I get to become the hands and feet of Jesus. In this way God is growing me and making me more like Him. With adoptees and adoptive parents, I can offer what I was rarely given: understanding from someone who has been there.

The apostle Peter wrote, "Each of you should use whatever gift you have received to serve others, as faithful stewards of God's grace in its various forms" (1 Peter 4:10). In our broken world, sometimes the "gifts" that we receive are our deepest wounds, which become healed and used by God as ministry tools. The very things that almost destroyed us become the things God uses to bring life to others.

The Ministry Expands

As I began sharing more openly, the opportunities for God to use my story have multiplied. One avenue He has opened, for which I am extremely grateful and which is the reason for this book you are currently holding, is that of writing. I started writing this book out of obedience, to relate experiences from my adoption and the lifelong journey God and I have shared. Then I started a blog about my thoughts on adoption from a Christian perspective: "Roxanne's Thoughts Along the Way," which at the time of this writing can be found on Substack. There's nothing fancy about either; they are simply representations of my honest reflections on how I've found God in the adoption journey.

Along the way on the writing journey and the practice of my faith in general, the challenge has become integrating my adoption ministry with whole-life discipleship. I want to first be a follower of Christ who also happens to deeply understand adoption. To get to this point, I have been intentional to grow in all areas of my faith. Feelings of abandonment are one set of emotions I regularly bring before God, but there are others that God regularly speaks to me about too. Being an adoptee is not my only identity.

That being said, I recognize the special ways I am uniquely equipped to use adoption as a bridge to sharing the Gospel, and I don't avoid those. Sometimes there is a clear sense that God has brought someone into my life and they are wrestling with their identity or their concept of God as Father. Because of my situation and the ways God has spoken to me about these topics, I believe it's my responsibility to share from the ministry tools God has allowed into my life.

Generational Impact

One of the sweetest ministries has been opportunities God gives me within my family. My grandchildren are growing up with a grandmother whose adoption story is one of redemption, not shame. They know that families are formed by more than blood. They see adoption as one of the ways God builds families.

I also hope they understand the work God has done to break generational struggles. When Maggie placed Lynne and me up for adoption, she took the first step to moving two of her offspring out of the difficult situation she found herself and her other children in. Even though she didn't know what situation I may have been born into, my mother raised me in a healthy environment, and that has brought me to the place I am today, where I am able to invest what God has done into my grandchildren.

Kathryn: A Birth Mother's Perspective

It was Friday the 13th in Lynchburg, Virginia when Kathryn's life changed in a moment. She stared at the two pink lines on the stick and realized she was pregnant. Even though she was engaged to the baby's father, Armando, he had left to travel back to Mexico recently, and she couldn't imagine raising a baby without his support. For a brief moment, Kathryn considered abortion, but when she learned that the cost of the abortion was one thousand dollars, and she had no money or insurance, she knew that wasn't an option. From that point on, she planned to place the baby up for adoption.

Twenty years old, with a fiancee who had seemed to have disappeared, about to lose her job and her apartment, and now pregnant, Kathryn felt like she had few choices. She told two close friends about the pregnancy and decided to keep it a secret from everyone in her family, even her mother, whom she moved back in with. Several factors worked well for the decision to keep the pregnancy hidden. She never had morning sickness, and her six foot tall frame allowed her to hide her growing belly. Although she didn't visit a doctor for prenatal care, Kathryn took vitamins and tried to eat well so the baby would be healthy.

Two weeks before her twenty-first birthday, she woke at 5:30 a.m. with cramps but still went to work. From there she called a friend, who suspected Kathryn was in labor and came to drive her to the hospital. She was so successful at hiding her pregnancy that even the hospital staff needed to confirm the pregnancy through a test. When there was no doubt that not only was she pregnant, but she was in active labor, her friend fetched Kathryn's mother, who quickly came to the hospital. Their meeting at the hospital was emotional now that the secret of the pregnancy was out in the open.

After fifteen and a half hours, with her mother beside her, Kathryn delivered a healthy baby girl. In those early hours after delivery, someone handed her brochures for adoption agencies. She chose the Liberty Godparent Home, even though she wasn't following their typical adoption process, which involved mothers living at the home during pregnancy. Kathryn told the agency she wanted her daughter to be placed with a family who went to church, valued education, and encouraged sports.

The agency presented Kathryn with three profiles to consider. As she thought about her decision, and while the match was being made, the baby lived in foster care. When the chosen couple arrived to receive the baby, Kathryn stayed in another room but was able to observe the couple and their interactions. She felt comfortable with what she saw, and the baby went to her forever home.

For the next four months, Kathryn went through the counseling which Liberty required. She never doubted the decision to give her daughter up for adoption, but she did grieve that loss. It took time to process those emotions, and Kathryn chose not to have more children.

Sixteen years later, Kathryn heard from her daughter, Kristen, through the adoption agency. When she and Kristen first spoke on the phone, their conversation lasted for hours. Then, a couple of years later, when Kristen turned eighteen, she flew to Virginia to meet her birth mother face to face. That's when she also met her grandparents and other relatives. When Kristen married, Kathryn attended the wedding and met Kristen's adoptive parents. Now, when she visits Florida, they all share meals together as one extended family.

Kathryn has no regrets about placing Kristen and is proud of the woman she has become. Through Kristen's research, she finally learned what happened to Armando, Kristen's birth father. On his journey back to Mexico, Armando had been killed in an auto accident. His brother reported he never made it back home, and they did not know about Kathryn.

Recently Kathryn has returned to attending church, a Baptist one like she had been raised in. With the help of a counselor, she is working through depression related to job stress. Kathryn's encouragement to women facing unplanned pregnancies is that adoption is a beautiful option. Many loving families long to adopt and have good homes to offer. There are many agencies that allow birth mothers to help choose the adoptive family. Open adoptions are common now, and in these situations, a child can grow up knowing both birth and adoptive families, loved from many sides.

The Truths I Want You to Know

If you're adopted, maybe you're still wrestling with your story, even after reading this book and others like it. Maybe new questions have been brought to mind, or maybe you're at peace with your adoption circumstances. Wherever you are in the adoption journey, these are the truths I want to emphasize at the end of this book:

Your timeline is your own. It took me seven decades to be "glad" that I was adopted. It might take you less time than this, or it might take more. The very description of "glad" might be different for you. Whatever word you use, my prayer is that you have peace in your adoption, no matter how long it takes to find it.

Your feelings are valid. All of them. The anger, the grief, the confusion, the gratitude, the fear, the hope. All of these are important to feel and examine. Don't let anyone minimize or invalidate your emotions.

Your background story matters. Whether you decide to search for your birth family or not, whether you discover beauty or pain, whether your adoption was necessary or seemingly random—your story matters. There is no substitute for knowing your story, and you have the right to know your origin story.

Your wounds can heal. Deep wounds, like those that occur with adoption, usually leave scars. Those scars will heal and become less obvious over time. That doesn't mean they go away completely, but they hurt less, and then our wounds become part of our identity, our testimony.

You are not alone. In this book you've read just a sampling of adoption stories, and I hope that you understand you are not alone in this journey. You are in good company not only by the very fact of being adopted, but also in your pain and the questions that you carry. Others have walked this path, and God never leaves you alone.

Truths for Those Touched by Adoption

Although this book has been targeted to those who have been adopted, I don't want to ignore readers who have played a different role in adoption. You have loved and sacrificed much and also carry an important story.

To Birth Parents: Your courage in choosing life deserves recognition. Your grief is real and valid. Your child's gladness doesn't diminish your loss, but perhaps it can bring some comfort. You gave more than you know.

To Adoptive Parents: Thank you for saying yes to complexity. You have sacrificed and held steady as children have tested boundaries and explored the depths of your love. Along the way, you've learned that love doesn't fix everything, but you offered it anyway. You are seen and appreciated.

To Siblings and Extended Family: You matter too. It's no small thing to adjust to an adopted family member, and your place in the story counts. Thank you for making room, for sharing your parents, for being part of the journey.

Your Journey: Adoption as Insight to Spiritual Formation

No matter what your relationship with adoption is, the concept of adoption is a profound lens for faith. If you are an adoptee, you especially have insights into the feelings and experiences of living with the complicated emotions of being chosen and loved by adoptive parents. This is in fact reality for all Christians. We are chosen by God, and as we become sanctified, we come to understand in deeper ways the beauty of living as a child of God.

Through the unique situation of adoption, God brings insight into five aspects of relationship to which you as an adoptee can add the perspective of your life experience and wisdom.

1. Being **chosen**: "For he chose us in him before the creation of the world to be holy and blameless in his sight" (Ephesians 1:4).
2. **Identified** as a child of God: "Yet to all who did receive him, to those who believed in his name, he gave the right to become children of God" (John 1:12).
3. **Belonging** to God's family: "But now this is what the Lord says—he who created you…'Do not fear, for I have redeemed you; I have summoned you by name; you are mine'" (Isaiah 43:1).
4. Unearned **grace** is ours: "For it is by grace you have been saved, through faith—and this is not from yourselves, it is the gift of God—not by works, so no one can boast" (Ephesians 2:8-9).
5. We have been **redeemed** even more ways than spiritual: "For he has rescued us from the dominion of darkness and brought us into the kingdom of the Son he loves, in whom we have redemption, the forgiveness of sins" (Colossians 1:13-14).

A Simple Four-Stage Movement

As you recognize the ways God has equipped you to minister to others out of your adoption experiences, be sure to not skip over your own healing. This doesn't mean God can't use your experiences until He has brought you fully through to a place of acceptance, but it is important not to skip over the important work that needs to happen in your own life and heart before investing in others.

Throughout this book, I've encouraged you to be honest about your feelings. Sit with them and examine the places that still are tender. This healing will bring restoration to your own heart and also allows you to heal in your community and relationships with those who may have hurt you.

Healing doesn't happen all at once. Sometimes God reveals aspects of our hurt and various feelings one at a time. As these emotions surface, look at each one and process how it relates to the story you already are living. If you learn new information through your search for your biological family, processing will be important to integrate pieces of your story that are new.

When God brings people into your life who are hurting, look for how He wants you to help them. Maybe He will use insights you've gained along the way to impart wisdom. It could be that you are a crucial listener that will sit with another person and be a support even through difficult times.

Adoption ministry is going to be a valuable place where God will use your wisdom and experiences. At the same time, be aware of letting the experience of adoption define your entire identity. No one is shaped by any single thing, and this is no different for adoptees. Yes, all of the aspects of your adoption are key to understanding what God has done in your life, but He uses many other situations in each of our lives as well. God's design is complex, and His children are shaped using a variety of His tools.

Reflection Moment

1. What season of discipleship are you in: early healing, active processing, ready to help, or integrated ministry?
2. What unique gifts does your adoption story give you?
3. Where might God use your story: in formal ministry, informal support, professional work, or family legacy?
4. What preparation do you still need: further healing, education, community support, or practical training?
5. How can adoption inform but not define your ministry?

Significant Next Steps

Are you ready to step into opportunities to use your spiritual experiences as a way to encourage others? It's okay if you're not ready. Healing takes years, and rushing through it and being half-hearted is never a good idea. If you're not ready to explore the ways God is going to use your adoption story yet, feel free to skip past this section and on to the next chapter.

Get Equipped. Read widely on adoption, on healing, on the issues many adoptees wrestle with, and attend conferences. Build your support system. I suggest finding three key people to be part of your network. Look for one adoptee earlier in the journey of processing, one adoptive parent who needs support, and one birth parent carrying grief. Reach out to them, listen, and care. You'll build valuable experience and begin the practice of ministry.

During this preparation stage, many people find it helpful to create a ministry mission statement. It could start with, "God has called me to use my adoption story to..." Successful mission statements are specific, flexible, measurable, and sustainable.

Test the Waters. Look for small opportunities to begin. Offer to share your testimony at church, lead one support meeting, or write an article for a newsletter, blog, or magazine.

Curate your testimony to fit a variety of situations. You may want to practice a two-minute version for casual sharing, a ten-minute version for groups, and a thirty-minute version for events. Practice until it feels natural.

Create Boundaries. Decide what to share, protect family privacy, set limits on availability, and maintain non-adoption related interests.

Build Slowly. Begin with one-to-one ministry, then small groups, then larger platforms, if that's where God leads.

Prayer

Dear God,

Thank You that You are a God of redemption. You take my adoption story, remind me of your love for me, and give me courage to share this grace with others.

Please prepare me and show me how to steward this story faithfully. Keep me from hiding it in shame or exploiting it for attention. Grant wisdom to know when to speak and when to listen, when to lead and when to follow, when to share my story and when to hold sacred space for someone else.

Root me in Your love as Your child above all else. Give me endurance for the race before me. Keep me from rushing ahead of Your timing or lagging behind in fear. Give me courage to follow and humility to serve.

Thank You that no part of my story is wasted. May my life be a bridge that others can cross to find You.

Amen.

A Final Thought

When I was sixteen at that concert, I had no idea that the God who saved me would one day use every part of my story, even the parts I wanted to hide. I never imagined that my questions about identity would help others find theirs in Christ. This is the beauty of God's economy. He doesn't waste anything. Whether it's our adoption journeys or any of the other trials we face in life, God has power and delights to use it all.

Your ministry may not look like mine. You may not write or speak publicly. You may minister through the way you raise your children to understand adoption, the way you support adoptive families in crisis, the way you live with integrity in complex family systems, the way you notice outsiders and bring them in, or the way you quietly mentor one person at a time.

Size does not matter. Visibility does not matter. Faithfulness matters. Take what God has given you, including your adoption story, and use it for His glory and for the good of others. Your adoption prepared you for ministry in ways you are still discovering. It's a journey toward wholeness, and God gives us the privilege to help others along the way. This is what lifelong discipleship looks like.

Snapshots of Grace

The best thing about a picture is that it never changes, even when the people in it do.

ANDY WARHOL

SOMETIMES WE CAN DISCOVER the most profound truths through a visual image. I love photographs because I often wonder about the moments surrounding that captured split second. What was happening in the moments before and after the flash burst? Did the smiles disappear immediately after the moment passed? I've chosen to add a chapter of photographs because I want you to have the same opportunity to wonder.

These snapshots from my journey and the journeys of others are external demonstrations of how God weaves beauty from brokenness, wholeness from wounds, and family from fragments.

As you look at these images, see not just the people in them, but the grace that brought us all together. Picture yourself in the stories these images show, and know God has been near to you through every moment of your life whether images of your past might have shown you with a smile or sadness in your eyes.

Roxanne three days old coming home from the hospital

George, Rosemary, and Roxanne

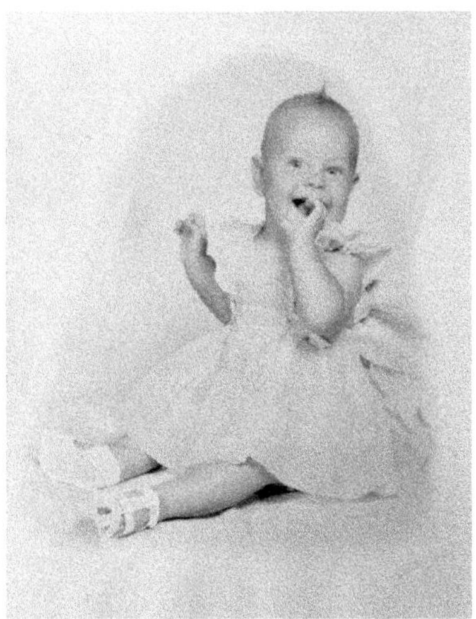

Toddler Roxanne

Roxanne and her dog, Mitzi

Roxanne's birth mother, Maggie

Roxanne with maternal grandparents, James & May

Roxanne with Grandpa James

Godparents Frank & Anna Hoare

Rosemary and Dave

Tommy

Baby picture of Roxanne's younger son

Tommy and younger brother

Roxanne & Noel's wedding day

Roxanne & Noel, Alaska, 2023

Roxanne and Noel, 30th anniversary

Roxanne meets Aunt Ardith & Norval

Roxanne's four siblings (Robert, Ardith, Amber, & Tommy)

Roxanne and Amber

(L to R) Cousins Nancy & Ardie Ruth, Aunt Ardith,
Roxanne & Amber

Roxanne and Aunt Ardith

Roxanne & Noel's blended family

Appendix

RESOURCES FOR YOUR JOURNEY

Plans fail for lack of counsel, but with many advisers they succeed.

PROVERBS 15:22

Your journey toward wholeness doesn't end with the last page of this book—it continues with every step you take toward healing, understanding, and purpose. This appendix provides practical resources to support you wherever you are on your adoption journey. Whether you're just beginning to process your story or you're ready to help others with theirs, these tools can guide your next steps.

Remember: You don't have to walk this path alone. God has provided helpers, healers, and hope for every part of your journey.

Support Organizations and Communities

National Organizations

National Council for Adoption: adoptioncouncil.org

Online Communities

Adoptee Rights Campaign

- Facebook group with 10,000+ members
- Advocacy and support
- Search assistance

How Does It Feel to Be Adopted

- Private Facebook group
- Safe space for processing feelings
- Adoptees only

Search and Reunion Support

Ancestry.com

- DNA testing
- Family trees

DNAadoption.org

- Methodology for using DNA to find family

- Classes and tools
- Success stories

International Soundex Reunion Registry (ISRR)

- Website: isrr.org
- Free mutual consent registry
- Matches adoptees with searching birth family

Professional Support

Finding Adoption-Competent Therapy

What to Look For:

- Specific training in adoption issues
- Understanding of the Seven Core Issues of adoption
- Trauma-informed approach
- No agenda about searching or not searching
- Validates your experience without minimizing

Questions to Ask Potential Therapists:

1. What training do you have specific to adoption?
2. How many adoptees have you worked with?
3. What's your view on birth family searches?
4. Are you familiar with adoption trauma?
5. Do you understand the difference between confidential and open adoption impacts?

Therapy Directories:

- Psychology Today (filter for adoption)
- EMDR International Association (for trauma)
- American Association of Christian Counselors

Specialized Therapeutic Approaches

EMDR (Eye Movement Desensitization and Reprocessing) is particularly effective for:

- Pre-verbal trauma
- Attachment injuries
- Traumatic reunion experiences

Brainspotting helps process:

- Deep emotional wounds
- Body-held trauma
- Identity confusion

Internal Family Systems (IFS) are useful for:

- Integrating different parts of identity
- Healing the "exile" of the rejected child
- Building self-compassion

Practical Exercises for Your Journey

Daily Practices

Morning Identity Affirmation - Start each day with truth:

- "I am chosen by God and by people"
- "My story has purpose"
- "I am whole, even with questions"
- "I belong to God's family forever"

Evening Gratitude Practice - End each day naming:

- One thing about your adoption story you're grateful for
- One person who showed you love today
- One way you saw God's hand in your story

Weekly Reflection Questions

- **Monday:** What am I feeling about my adoption this week?
- **Tuesday:** Where did I see God's protection in my past?
- **Wednesday:** What question do I need to bring to God today?
- **Thursday:** Who in my life needs to hear "me too" about adoption?
- **Friday:** What healing step can I take this weekend?
- **Saturday:** How can I celebrate my story today?

- **Sunday:** What scripture speaks to my adoptee heart this week?

Monthly Growth Challenges

- **Month 1:** Write your adoption story in 500 words. Focus on facts, not feelings.
- **Month 2:** Write your adoption story again, this time focusing only on feelings.
- **Month 3:** Write your adoption story from God's perspective.
- **Month 4:** Interview an adoptive parent (yours or someone else's) about their experience.
- **Month 5:** Connect with one adoption support group (online or in-person).
- **Month 6:** Create an "adoption gratitude list" with 50 items.
- **Month 7:** Write letters you'll never send—to birth parents, adoptive parents, yourself.
- **Month 8:** Research your cultural heritage (birth or adoptive) and embrace one tradition.
- **Month 9:** Share your story with one safe person who doesn't know it.
- **Month 10:** Create art expressing your adoption journey (painting, collage, music, poetry).
- **Month 11:** Volunteer with an adoption-related organization.
- **Month 12:** Write your testimony of God's faithfulness in your adoption story.

Scripture for the Journey

For Identity

- Ephesians 1:4-5 (Chosen before the foundation of the world)
- Isaiah 43:1 (Called by name)
- 1 John 3:1 (What manner of love)
- Psalm 139:13-16 (Fearfully and wonderfully made)

For Abandonment Fears

- Deuteronomy 31:6 (He will never leave you)
- Isaiah 49:15-16 (Engraved on His palms)
- Romans 8:38-39 (Nothing can separate us)
- Hebrews 13:5 (Never will I leave you)

For Purpose

- Jeremiah 29:11 (Plans to prosper you)
- Romans 8:28 (All things work together)
- Ephesians 2:10 (Created for good works)
- Esther 4:14 (For such a time as this)

For Healing

- Psalm 147:3 (He heals the brokenhearted)
- Isaiah 61:1-3 (Beauty for ashes)
- 2 Corinthians 5:17 (New creation)
- Revelation 21:5 (Making all things new)

Creating Your Personal Support Plan

Step 1: Assess Your Needs

Rate each area from 1-10 (10 being fully resourced):

- Emotional support: ____
- Spiritual guidance: ____
- Professional therapy: ____
- Adoption education: ____
- Community connection: ____
- Search support: ____
- Family relationships: ____

Step 2: Identify Your Gaps

Where did you score 5 or below? These are your priority areas.

Step 3: Choose Your Next Steps

For each gap area, select ONE resource from this chapter to explore this month.

Step 4: Build Your Team

You need:

- A counselor (professional support)
- A confessor (spiritual support)
- A companion (peer support)
- A cheerleader (encouragement)

Step 5: Track Your Progress

Keep a simple journal noting:

- Resources tried
- What helped
- What didn't
- Next steps

Starting Your Own Support Group

Sometimes the best resource is the one you create. If your area lacks adoption support:

Getting Started

1. **Pray first** - Ask God to guide and provide
2. **Start small** - Even 2-3 people is enough
3. **Meet consistently** - Monthly is sustainable
4. **Create safety** - Confidentiality is crucial
5. **Share leadership** - Prevent burnout

Meeting Structure (2 hours)

- Welcome and guidelines (10 min)
- Check-in round (30 min)
- Topic discussion or speaker (45 min)
- Open sharing (30 min)
- Closing prayer/encouragement (5 min)

Topic Ideas

- Dealing with birthdays
- Mother's Day/Father's Day survival
- Search and reunion experiences
- Talking to kids about adoption
- Setting boundaries with family
- Finding identity in Christ
- Handling adoption questions
- Celebrating adoption positives

A Personal Resource Library

Consider building a collection of resources you can return to and share:

Essential Documents

- This book's exercises completed
- Your written adoption story (multiple versions)
- Scripture cards for difficult days
- Contact list of support people
- Therapy notes and insights
- Timeline of your healing journey

Creative Resources

- Playlist of songs that speak to your journey
- Photos that document your story
- Art that expresses your feelings
- Quotes that encourage you
- Prayers you've written

- Letters (sent and unsent)

For Sharing Your Story

When you're ready to help others:

Speaking Opportunities

- Church testimony
- Adoption support groups
- Youth groups
- Counseling centers
- Adoption agencies
- Conferences

Writing Opportunities

- Blog about your journey
- Submit articles to adoption magazines
- Write your full memoir
- Create devotionals for adoptees
- Share on social media
- Guest post on adoption websites

Ministry Opportunities

- Mentor newer adoptees
- Support adoptive families in crisis
- Advocate for adoption reform
- Pray for adoption triad members
- Start an adoption ministry at church
- Volunteer with foster care

Your Next Step

Look back through this chapter. Circle THREE resources that spoke to your heart. Don't overwhelm yourself with trying everything. Just pick three:

1. One book to read
2. One group to join
3. One practice to start

Write them here:
    Book I'll read: _______________________________
    Group I'll join: _______________________________
    Practice I'll start: _____________________________
    By this date: ________________________________

A Final Resource: Prayer

The greatest resource you have is direct access to the God who orchestrated your story. Here's a prayer to use whenever you need it:

Faithful Father,

Thank You for resources—for books that understand, people who care, and tools that heal. Thank You that I don't have to figure this out alone.

Guide me to the resources I need right now. Not everything, just what's next. Give me wisdom to know what to read, who to trust, and when to rest.

Help me remember that You are my ultimate resource. When human helpers fail, You remain. When books don't have answers, You are still Truth. When groups can't meet my needs, You are sufficient.

Use me as a resource for others. Let my healing help someone else heal. Let my story point to Yours.

In Jesus' name, who knows what it means to be adopted by an earthly father,

Amen.

Remember: Resources are tools, not saviors. They point us toward healing, but Jesus is the Healer. They offer community, but God is our belonging. They provide information, but the Holy Spirit gives wisdom.

Use these resources. Share them freely. Add to them as you discover new helps along the way. And always remember—the fact that you're seeking resources means you're already on the journey toward wholeness.

That's worth celebrating.

Epilogue

THE INVITATION

Now, at the end of the book, here's my invitation: Don't stop where you are. Keep walking. Keep processing. Keep healing. Keep seeking. Keep asking God to reveal His purposes in your story.

God doesn't waste any part of your journey. He's the master of taking what was meant for harm and using it for good. He's in the business of redeeming stories. Your adoption is not a mistake to be fixed or a tragedy to be survived. It's a story being written by One who doesn't write boring stories. He only writes epics of redemption.

A Prayer for Your Journey

Adoptive Father,

Thank You for this reader who has walked with me through these pages. You know exactly where they are on their journey. For those still wounded, be the Healer. For those still searching, be the Guide. For those still angry, be the Peace. For those still grieving, be the Comfort. For those finding gladness, be the Joy.

Show them that their adoption story is held within Your larger adoption story—that You chose them before the foundation of the world, that You pursued them relentlessly, that You paid the ultimate price to make them Yours.

Give them courage for the next step, whatever it is.

Most of all, remind them that they are Yours—twice chosen, deeply loved, eternally held.

May they someday say, in their own way and time, "I'm glad for my story, because it led me to You."

In the name of Jesus, who knows what it means to be adopted by an earthly father and to adopt us into an eternal family,

Amen.

One Final Truth

As a child, I never dreamed that one day, as an adult, I would realize how glad I was to be adopted. Not everyone reading this book will arrive at the same belief, because each of us has our own unique experience as an adoptee.

I have come to recognize the significant part God has played in our adoption journey, moving us closer to wholeness and healing. The discovery that God loves us and has a plan for us significantly impacts and changes our lives.

We may have been given up by our birth parents, but our heavenly Father has always watched over and cared for us as we grew up to become who we are today. You have been shaped by everything you have experienced in life, and your adoption is just one part.

My hope is that my book will be a catalyst to help you examine your feelings and emotions as you begin to experience healing. Our goal is to be whole and to share our own adoption journey with others. If this book helps even one adoptee, then the years of writing, re-writing, and editing will be worth the effort. My prayer is to encourage other adoptees by sharing my own personal stories.

With love and hope for your journey,
Roxanne

He has made everything beautiful in its time.

ECCLESIASTES 3:11

Acknowledgments

It takes a combined effort of many people to make the publication of your first book a reality. My loving husband Noel has encouraged me these past few years as I've worked on this book. I am thankful for his love, commitment, and understanding, which have sustained me as I discovered and developed my love of writing. Jeff Miller, my writing coach, taught and inspired me and has been a faithful friend. He and his wonderful team have loved, supported, and encouraged me on this writing journey. My editor, Angie; Abigail, the editor and layout expert; Tia, the graphic designer; and Chris, the book launcher all worked together to help me reach the finish line.

My fellow writers in our Tuesday writing class offered suggestions to make this book a resource that would support and speak to adoptees and their families. If even one person is helped, then all my hard work will be worth the effort.

Many thanks go to the adoptees, adoptive parents, siblings, family members, and a birth mother who all willingly told their stories and personal thoughts. I believe readers will be blessed by what they all shared.

I am thankful and give the glory to my Lord Jesus for saving me and showing me the way I should go, and also for His precious Holy Spirit that inspires me daily. My cohort knows that when the Spirit moves, Roxanne writes!

Roxanne Taylor was born in 1954 and raised in Florida, adopted at birth and brought up as an only child. Later in life, her journey of discovery led her to reconnect with her birth family, where she learned she had five older siblings—an unexpected gift that deepened her understanding of identity, belonging, and grace.

Her strong and mature Christian faith has shaped her life and her writing. In 2022, Roxanne began putting words to her story, guided by a Christian writing coach and supported by a writing community. This journey gave birth to her Substack blog, *Roxanne's Thoughts Along the Way*, and eventually to this book.

Her debut, *I'm Glad I Was Adopted: A Journey to Wholeness and Faith* (Indie Christian Book, 2026), shares her personal story with honesty and hope. Written to encourage adoptees, their families, and anyone seeking wholeness in Christ, her book reminds readers that God's hand can be seen in every chapter of their lives.

At the time of this writing, Roxanne has been married to her husband, Noel, for thirty years. Together they share one son and three daughters and delight in their nine grandchildren. Now retired, they live in central Florida, where faith, family, and storytelling continue to shape their daily lives.

You can reach Roxanne at RoxannesThoughts@gmail.com.

S·E·A·
SOLDIER ENCHANCED ADAPTATION

KRIS MICHAEL MCKENNA
KA PLOUFFE

PP

Publishing Place LLC
WWW.PUBLISHINGPLACE.NET

S.E.A. | by Kris Michael McKenna & KA Plouffe

Copyright © 2026, Publishing Place LLC

Published in the United States by Publishing Place LLC, Skowhegan, Maine, United States

The 'PP' colophon are trademarks of Publishing Place LLC

ISBN: 978-1-969343-04-9 (*Paperback*)

LCCN: 2025927343

Printed in the United States of America

First Edition 2026.

Publishing Place
Skowhegan, ME 04976

www.publishingplace.net